The Western Guide to

FENG SHUI

for Prosperity

Also by Terah Kathryn Collins

Card Deck/Books

FENG SHUI PERSONAL PARADISE CARDS: Booklet and 54-Card Deck

THE WESTERN GUIDE TO FENG SHUI: Room by Room

HOME DESIGN WITH FENG SHUI A–Z

THE WESTERN GUIDE TO FENG SHUI:
Creating Balance, Harmony, and Prosperity in Your Environment

Audiocassettes

INTRODUCTION TO FENG SHUI

THE WESTERN GUIDE TO FENG SHUI
(6-tape audio program and workbook)

All of the above products are available at your local bookstore,
or by calling Hay House at: (800) 654-5126 • www.hayhouse.com

The Western Guide to

FENG SHUI

for Prosperity

True Accounts

of People

Who Have

Applied

Essential

Feng Shui

to Their Lives

and Prospered

TERAH KATHRYN COLLINS

Hay House, Inc.
Carlsbad, California • Sydney, Australia
Canada • Hong Kong • United Kingdom

Copyright © 2002 by Terah Kathryn Collins

Published and distributed in the United States by:
    Hay House, Inc., P.O. Box 5100, Carlsbad, CA 92018-5100 • (800) 654-5126
(800) 650-5115 (fax) • www.hayhouse.com
    Hay House Australia Pty Ltd, P.O. Box 515, Brighton-Le-Sands NSW 2216
phone: 1800 023 516 • *e-mail:* info@hayhouse.com.au

Editorial supervision: Jill Kramer • *Design:* Jenny Richards • *Illustrations:* Eris Klein

Library of Congress Cataloging-in-Publication Data

Collins, Terah Kathryn.
    Western guide to feng shui for prosperity / Terah Kathryn Collins.
        p. cm.
    ISBN 1-56170-813-5 (alk. paper)
     1. Feng shui. I. Title.

 BF1779.F4 C655 2002
 133.3'337--dc21

                                                                    2001051785

ISBN 1-56170-813-5

    05 04 03 02   4 3 2 1
        1st printing, April 2002

Printed in China by Palace Press International

Contents

Acknowledgments

If Pandora had opened the treasure chest that I opened in order to write this book, she would have been thrilled by who poured out. It's a chest filled with heavenly people of every persuasion, all of whom I wish to thank.

To Dr. Richard Tan, Louie Audet, and the many Feng Shui teachers who fan the Feng Shui fire within me: Thank you for your teachings and your willingness to share your knowledge.

To my two fabulous Feng Shui story scouts, Karen Carrasco and Terri Stark, who expertly gathered the "bones" of these stories from practitioners around the country: Thank you for your dedication not only to the work, but to making me laugh and enjoy the writing process more than ever before.

To Carolyn Bratton, Cynthia Crisp, Katharine Deleot, Don Fiore, BJ Gorman, Becky Iott, Christina Jantzen, Judy Lonn, Maria Mark, Judith Nourse, Ellen Schneider, Evelyn Seed, Martha Seidel, Pam Stutzman, Holly Tashian, Pauline Uhing, and Lainie Wrightson: Thank you for sharing the wealth of your Feng Shui experiences with me and for being the cornerstone of inspiration throughout this project.

To Jonathan Hulsh, co-founder of the Western School of Feng Shui and my soul brother: Thank you for working twice as hard while I finished this book, and for being a phenomenal partner and great friend. Congratulations and countless blessings on your marriage to Dr. Rabia Barkins. You two are good fortune in motion.

To my school staff: Jane Ozuna, Rita Cofrancesco, and Liv Kellgren. It's an honor to witness the exquisite work you do in serving our students and alumni, and a great pleasure to spend time with you. Thanks also to our Seminar Director, Karen Carrasco, for your brilliant ability to logistically maintain harmony at the practitioner trainings.

To our masterful Feng Shui teacher, Becky Iott: Thank you for blessing the school's practitioner training with your ability to imbue students with everything they need in order to become wise and effective practitioners. Your friendship and your Feng Shui expertise are pure grace in my life.

To the alumni of the school, thanks for transforming our world—home by home and business by business—into a place where harmony reigns.

Thanks to my publisher, Hay House, and all the good people there whose single focus is to inspire the world through the printed word—including Donna Abate, Shelley Anderson, Bryn Best, Jacqui Clark, Julie Davison, Lisa Kelm, Jill Kramer, Janice Lewis, Jeannie Liberati, Shannon Littrell, Robin Mayfield, Summer McStravick, Margarete Nielsen, Ashley Parsons, Jenny Richards, Christy Salinas, Adrian Sandoval, Chandra Teitscheid, Ron Tillinghast, Tonya Toone, and Reid Tracy. And to Louise Hay, thank you for being a guiding light for literally millions of people on the planet. You've certainly rocked my world!

To Eris Klein, a gifted artist whose illustrations capture more than words can say: You are a joy to work with.

To my friends who so generously fed me throughout this project— Laurel and Matthew Aarsvold, John Chase, Jennifer and David Cornsweet, Maria DePalma and Dennis Doyle, Gary DeRodriguez and Roger Mosser, Jackie and Richard Earnest, Tony and Kovida Fisher, Gita Gendloff and Sand Miller, Mary Lou LoPreste, Shivam and Apara Kohls, Barbara Masters and Alan Richards, Mary and John McGuiness, Marti and Ron Montbleau, Lisa Neely, Joan and Steve Ottoway, Francina and Neal Prince, Ellen and Billy Simms, and Barbara Takashima and Dan McFarland—thank you. Your kind generosity and friendship were the perfect antidote to a deadline.

And finally, to Brian Collins, my husband and soulmate, who essentially co-wrote this book with me. Thank you for holding the foundation of my personal life to your heart and co-creating with me a heavenly life.

Introduction

Feng Shui, the study of how to arrange your environment to enhance your life, is a virtual gold mine of opportunity for those who choose to practice it. For the last 12 years, I've mined the riches of my own experiences and distilled them into *Essential Feng Shui*, which focuses on the many practical applications that Feng Shui can have in our Western culture. My work has included the engaging and rewarding tasks of writing books, teaching, and establishing the Western School of Feng Shui. Each of these blessings has expanded my recognition and appreciation of the many ways in which Feng Shui can align us with our destinies.

This collection of true accounts focuses on the enhancement of wealth from a Feng Shui perspective. It's very exciting to bring you these stories, as they document what happens when an Essential Feng Shui practitioner introduces "this Fung Shooey stuff" to family, friends, and clients. Each "rags-to-riches" tale reveals a nugget of Feng Shui wisdom that can add richness to your own life. And since stories can be one of the most pleasant ways in which to learn, it's my hope that you'll be both entertained and inspired as you read.

While the real names of the practitioners are used in the stories, the identities, and often the professions, of clients have been changed to protect their privacy. All of the photographs, excerpts from journals, and hand-drawn maps were submitted by the practitioner or client. In addition, I've also included a Bagua Map and chart of the Five Elements, which are two indispensable Feng Shui tools that are frequently referred to throughout the book. (These can be found in the Appendices.)

In Feng Shui, *wealth* and *prosperity* are associated with much more than money—these words also represent the invaluable treasures that money can't buy, such as good health, loving relationships with friends and family, auspicious opportunities, creative self-expression, and a meaningful spiritual life. Even so, people in our culture often begin their Feng Shui journey focused strictly on increasing their financial well-being. To help them achieve this aim, the Feng Shui practitioner may refer to the Bagua Map (see page 167), and suggest enhancing the Wealth and Prosperity area, or other related places in the home. Other suggestions might include cultivating an attitude of gratitude, simplifying and organizing cluttered areas, adding environmental affirmations, or arranging furniture and belongings to encourage optimal Ch'i flow. The result is that the enhancement of people's homes or offices can enrich any facet of life that's "poor"; and in doing so, they often receive much more than money. Money is just one desirable thing on the endless list of valuables—the truly abundant life is brimming with experiences that nurture and sustain the body, heart, *and* soul.

How do you create a prosperous life? In Chinese, *Feng Shui* literally translates to "wind water," so it's as simple as understanding those two elements. *Wind,* the unseen force of nature, symbolizes the inner world of your thoughts, goals, feelings, and prayers. *Water,* the visible force of nature, represents the outer world, including your home and workplace. Like the natural forces of wind and water, your inner and outer worlds are constantly interacting with one another. Discordant interactions between the two yield unhappy, "stormy" times, while harmonious interactions produce joyous, "fair-weather" conditions in life. This relationship between the inner intention and outer environment is like gravity, in that it's happening all the time, whether you're aware of it or not. By acknowledging and working with the dynamic relationship between you and your surroundings, you can become your own "weather maker," and create the harmonious life that you seek.

In Feng Shui, a harmonious life is built upon a foundation of three principles.

1. The First Principle

The first principle states that everything in the world—including your home and all of its contents—is alive with the vital energy called *Ch'i.* When you view the world in this way, belongings such as furniture, artwork, kitchenware, clothing, and equipment are transformed from lifeless "stuff" into living things that stimulate specific thoughts, feelings, and memories. They're part of the seen world, and you can't move without receiving impressions from them that repeatedly strengthen or weaken your inner world. The well-being of your internal life (your "wind Ch'i") is constantly influenced by your responses to the outer world (your "water Ch'i"), especially in the intimate environment of your home. Possessions that hold negative associations keep that negativity alive and anchor unfortunate circumstances in place, while things infused with positive associations act as environmental affirmations that attract good fortune to your door. One of the keys to creating fair-weather conditions in life and attracting wealth is to surround yourself with the things that enrich you in some way—that uplift and strengthen you every time you see them.

2. The Second Principle

The second principle that holds a harmonious life in place says that, like threads in a global tapestry, we're all inextricably connected. The richer your bonds are with your relationships, your environment, and your possessions—or people, places, and things—the more truly prosperous your life will become. This principle encourages you to heal old wounds, speak the truth, and cultivate meaningful relationships with family, friends, and community. Knowing that everything is connected also emphasizes the importance of comfort, safety, and beauty in your surroundings. When you realize that the choices you make in your decor are linked to your success in the world, you can then create an extremely supportive environment—one that embraces and inspires *you*. You'll find yourself removing items that cause you emotional or physical irritation, injury, and discomfort; arranging furnishings to capture optimal views; and displaying personally meaningful tokens of beauty that keep your spirits lifted. All of these actions have one purpose: to graciously align and connect your highest intentions with your habitat so that good fortune and well-being are best assured.

3. The Third Principle

The third foundational principle is that everything is constantly changing. Change is your ally, for it's the force that can make your life better. You can realize your goals by making positive changes in your living space, which is a perfect example of blending wind (inner mind) and water (outer place) to achieve a favorable result. One of the best ways to encourage positive change is to simplify and organize your belongings. As you let go of excess and clear away clutter, you'll inevitably notice a rather magical consequence: Your wishes will start to come true because you've made space for enriching changes to take place. For instance, you may clean up a chaotic garage and receive a promotion the next week, or free a foyer from clutter and find that the spark that's been missing from your love life is magically rekindled. When the excess and clutter that prevented beneficial change from moving your life forward are eliminated, all heaven can break loose in your life.

These three principles describe a physical world where every person, place, and thing is alive, interconnected, and always changing. . . . We live in a dynamic world where everyone and everything matters, and where every moment is a potential bridge to a blessed future.

The stories in this book tell the tale—in each one, people joined forces with their surroundings. They set their intentions for positive change and then took action. They explored their connection with the things "who" are alive with life-affirming thoughts, feelings, memories, and associations. They simplified and organized their possessions; embraced change; and let comfort, safety, and beauty be fully expressed around them. And in every case, they discovered that the creation of a personal paradise was quite literally in their own hands.

Their stories invite you to make the very same discovery.

1

Gone Fishin'

Holly Tashian was faced with a tricky situation. Her friend Megan had asked her to apply her Feng Shui expertise to her husband's office. Holly knew that Nick, Megan's husband, didn't believe in "that Chinese stuff," and was only allowing her to consult with him because his wife insisted upon it.

Nick ran an advertising business that did very well—the only problem was that money poured out of the company as fast as it poured in. As a result, Nick was perpetually frazzled and agitated about work, and he had the bad habit of bringing all of this negative energy home with him every night. Megan was tired of it. She was worried about Nick's health and wanted Holly to "do her magic and fix it." Holly agreed to do so on the condition that she would not "force" Nick into anything. She'd take a look at his work space, talk with him, and see what happened.

Nick's company was located in a 6,000-square-foot office on the second floor of a prestigious downtown building. As Holly stepped off the elevator, her first impression was . . . *thirst.* The fiery colors of the Southwest were everywhere—walls in sunset colors were hung with paintings of desert scenes.

1

Clearly preoccupied, Nick met Holly in the reception area and took her on a quick tour. The Southwest theme carried on throughout the entire space, including the employees' offices. Holly noted that almost every office had the same Feng Shui challenge: While desks had been placed so that employees could see the door, there were floor-to-ceiling windows behind their chairs. *And so it begins*, Holly thought. *An excessive flow of energy is being pulled through the windows, taking prosperity along with it.*

As soon as they got to Nick's office, he had to take a phone call. This gave Holly a few minutes to look around. She immediately noticed that although his desk sat prominently in the room facing the door, the same floor-to-ceiling windows that were in the other offices were also located behind him. A desert painting and several Southwest artifacts decorated the gold walls—including a cow's skull that faced Nick's desk.

Nick motioned for Holly to take a seat in one of his red leather chairs, finished his call, and joined her. "I know Megan's worried about me," he volunteered, "and I don't blame her. I'm sick to death of running this place, and I'm going to get the hell out as soon as I can find someone to replace me."

Holly stared at him. "Now *there's* an attitude. It sounds like you're burned out, Nick." He agreed with a stiff nod of his head.

"May I start by rewording your objective?" Holly asked. He gave her an annoyed look, which she ignored. "How about . . . 'My intention is to train the perfect person to uphold the success and integrity of this company so that I may retire on or before June 30, 2000.'"

"Sounds like what I just said," Nick shot back. They both laughed, and he seemed to relax a little.

Holly pointed to the artwork and asked him to tell her about it.

"Everyone knows that's Death Valley. Came from one of our clients who manufactured Western wear. They've since gone out of business, or 'crashed and burned,' as we like to say." He paused and eyed Holly. "Don't tell me that this art has anything to do with me."

Holly held his stare. "You tell me. Feng Shui observes that your environment is talking to you *all the time*. Looks to me like things in your office are saying: 'Nick's crashing and burning in his own personal Death Valley. In fact, bleached bones are all that are left of him.'"

Nick grinned. "Megan told me you'd put your finger on something, and maybe you have. So, Ms. Feng Shui, what do you suggest?"

The first thing Holly proposed was to eliminate the painting and the skull. "You've got an overabundance of the Fire element in here—and in your entire office, as a matter of fact. Too much Fire produces emotional burnout; days full of 'putting out fires,' stress, and anger. Sound familiar?"

Nick was taking the skull down as Holly spoke. "Yep, you're right on." He pushed a button on the phone for his secretary and said, "Come in here for a minute, I've got something for you." When she entered the room, he handed her the skull, saying, "Get rid of this thing, would you, please?" Too surprised to say anything, the secretary left the room holding the skull at arm's length.

Holly continued. "Okay, so all we have to do now is balance the elements in your office, decide what inspirational art to hang on the walls, put something between your back and those giant windows so that your money stays put and you feel supported for a change, and choose a personal symbol for your wealth area." [See Figure 1A.] She paused for a breath.

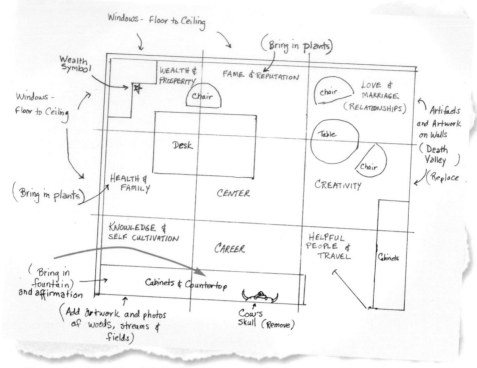

Figure 1A: *Bagua Map of Nick's office.*

Nick rolled his eyes. "Oh, is that all!"

Holly assured him that it wouldn't take long, and that any suggestions she would have for changes would have to meet with his approval.

He acquiesced, and an hour later, Nick ushered Holly back to the elevators with this list in his hand:

1. *Remove desert painting from my office and replace with framed enlargements of my river photographs. (Review photos from fishing trip and choose three; have Megan enlarge and frame them.)*

2. *Remove desert paintings/Southwest decor from reception, conference room, and*

hallways. Replace with art depicting woods and water. Ask Megan to help make choices. Do the same with employees' offices.

3. Buy plants and ceramic pots to go in front of office windows. For window behind desk, place plants behind chair (protection). Holly suggests one six-foot bamboo palm or ficus tree and two smaller plants per window (Megan).

4. Buy plants and ceramic pots for employees' windows, as above (Megan).

5. Purchase water feature made out of metal for countertop left of door. Look in nurseries, gift stores (Megan).

6. Write down intention and place under water feature.

7. Choose a symbol of wealth to display in back left corner on bookshelves—can be anything that symbolizes wealth to me (ask Megan).

Megan talked to Holly a couple of weeks later. "I've certainly been busy, thank you very much," she teased. "I let Nick make me his personal shopper because I knew it would never get done otherwise. But I've got to tell you, he's really calmed down. I swear he's a new man. And I don't know what you said to make him take that skull down—I've been after him for years to get rid of that nasty thing."

Holly asked about the office's other enhancements, and Megan filled her in on how happy everybody was to receive new plants and eliminate the Southwest theme. She had found a brass water feature for Nick's office and one for the reception area as well. "Plus," she said, "Nick's all proud because we're turning the office into a photo gallery of his work. The pictures will be back from the framers next week."

Holly was surprised when, about a month later, Nick telephoned. "Since when are you making social calls?" she asked.

"Since now . . . except this isn't a social call, it's business. I just want you to know that the voodoo you did in my office worked. [See Figure 1B.] I've got this smart kid I'm training to take over so I can get out of here. He's been working for me for a while, but it's only been since you came and jinxed the place that I realized he was my man. In fact, everything's a cool drink of water around here, to the point that I wonder if I'm in the same office. And, as you predicted, our profits aren't 'flying out the window' anymore."

As he spoke, Holly's heart was pounding. "Tell me something. What did you end up using as a wealth symbol in your office?"

Nick chuckled. "You're going to love this—I decided that I felt richest when I was fishing. So, I put a fancy little fake goldfish on my fishing pole and propped it up in the corner. Now it looks like I'm going to be fishing full time, right on schedule."

Postscript: Nick is now happily retired.

Figure 1B: *Nick's office includes a personally chosen Wealth enhancement and the balanced influences of the Five Elements. Large plants in ceramic pots provide some much-needed protection behind his desk chair, and his handwritten intention placed under the fountain holds his goal to retire in place.*

My intention is to train the perfect person to uphold the success and integrity of this company so that I may retire on or before June 30th, 2000.

Summary

Nick's office is a great example of what happens when one of the five elements dominates a space [see Appendix II]. Elemental extremes in the environment often cause behavioral extremes. In Nick's office, emotional stress, impatience, and aggressive behavior ruled—which are all signs of too much Fire. He and his employees felt "burned out" and "hot under the collar" most of the time. Although the element of Water is classically used to douse an overabundance of Fire, Holly's goal was to balance the five elements in Nick's surroundings to create an attractive and supportive environment. Holly helped him achieve this by suggesting the removal of some of the fiery decor and adding inspirational enhancements that introduced more of the Water, Wood, and Metal elements [see Figure 1B] to this "fiery" space. The Earth element was already well represented by the gold walls and the rectangular shape of the desk and other furniture. Holly also made sure that Nick's goals were actively held in place by his personally chosen wealth symbol and handwritten intention.

Feng Shui Tip

As in Nick's case, when there are large windows behind you, place something substantial between them and you—examples are plants, furniture, or window treatments. This honors our instinctual need for safety and comfort by providing support and protection from behind. It also helps to correct an excessive flow of energy through the room.

Nick's Feng Shui Enhancements

- ◈ Removal and replacement of fiery art and skull with nature photos.

- ◈ Placement of plants in front of large windows.

- ◈ Water fountain and written intention in Career area.

- ◈ Personal wealth symbol—a fishing pole and faux fish.

2

Law and a New Order

Maria Mark's Feng Shui journey began with an unexpected and most welcome gift— she became pregnant. [See Figure 2A.] It was a miracle that prompted a deep sense of gratitude as well as some serious soul-searching.

"I knew that my baby was going to change everything. I wanted to be a full-time mom for at least the first year, and then return to work part-time. I had been a paralegal for 15 years, and this meant that the career I'd been pursuing would have to come to an end, at least on some level, and that was fine with me. I felt like I was ending one life and beginning another, very different one. It was exciting and scary at the same time."

Maria's husband, Bob, was well aware of her metamorphosis, and he looked for ways to support and inspire her. Browsing through a bookstore one day, he came upon a display of books on a subject he'd never heard of before—Feng Shui. He thumbed

Figure 2A: *Maria at her baby shower.*

9

through several of them and realized that this was right up Maria's alley.

That night, Bob pressed a book into his wife's hands, declaring, "This Fung Shooey stuff sounds just like you."

He was right. As Maria consumed the book, she had an epiphany. She realized that she was a Feng Shui natural.

"After the baby's a year old," she announced, "I'm going to become a practitioner."

Garrett was born in June of 1999 [see Figure 2B], and during that year of full-time motherhood, Maria never lost sight of her goal to study Feng Shui. Shortly after Garrett celebrated his first birthday [see Figure 2C], she attended her first Feng Shui practitioner class.

June 7, 2000

> *My Dearest Garrett,*
>
> *You are soon to be one year old and what a year we have had! You have taught me so much about being responsible for someone else; about focusing my attention on someone other than myself; of caring for someone more than I've ever cared for anyone else (other than your father); and most of all, loving someone uncondi-tionally! You, my wonderful son, have taught me so much in our first year together, that I'm looking for-ward to the next year! I hope I pass this year!!*
>
> *Your student and tutor,*
>
> *Mom*

"I also decided to see if I could work part-time for my former employer and was told that they were only interested in full-time employees," Maria explains now. "This prompted me to use my own life as part of my Feng Shui

Figure 2B: *Maria holds her son, Garrett.*

June 7, 2000

My dearest Garrett,
    You are soon to be one year old and what a year we have had! You have taught me me so much about being responsible for someone else; about focusing my attention on someone other than myself; of caring for someone more than I've ever cared for anyone else (other than your father); and most of all, loving someone unconditionally! You, my wonderful son, have taught me so much in our first year together, that I'm looking forward to the next year! I hope I pass this year!!

Your student & tutor,

Mom

Figure 2C: *Maria's letter to her son, Garrett, on his first birthday. The letter is reprinted on page 10 so that you may clearly read Maria's words.*

homework. I was going to apply my new skills to create the perfect job for me."

Using the Bagua Map [see Appendix I], Maria focused on the areas of her home related to Career, Fame and Reputation, and Wealth and Prosperity [see Figure 2D].

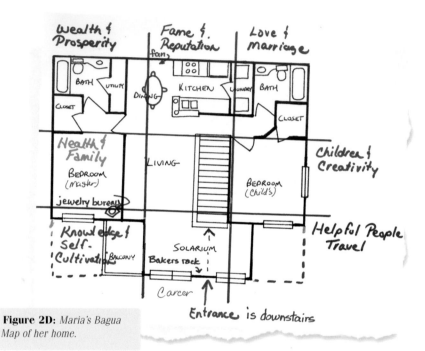

Figure 2D: *Maria's Bagua Map of her home.*

"My Career area was in my solarium, so there I placed a black baker's rack [see Figure 2E], which correlated with the elemental color associated with career. I decorated it with a black water fountain and my favorite career-related books—including those on Feng Shui, spirituality, and parenting. Then I accented either side of the baker's rack with plants to symbolize a flourishing new career.

"In the Fame and Reputation area, located in the dining room, I added red candles to the dining table and hung a red fan [see Figure 2F] on the wall to symbolize the illumination and heavenly unfolding of professional opportunities."

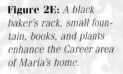

Figure 2E: *A black baker's rack, small fountain, books, and plants enhance the Career area of Maria's home.*

Figure 2F: *In the dining room, a large red fan brightens the area of the home related to Fame and symbolizes the heavenly unfolding of professional opportunities.*

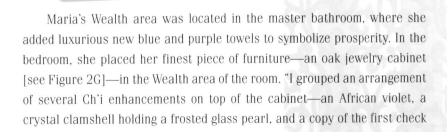

Maria's Wealth area was located in the master bathroom, where she added luxurious new blue and purple towels to symbolize prosperity. In the bedroom, she placed her finest piece of furniture—an oak jewelry cabinet [see Figure 2G]—in the Wealth area of the room. "I grouped an arrangement of several Ch'i enhancements on top of the cabinet—an African violet, a crystal clamshell holding a frosted glass pearl, and a copy of the first check

13

I'd received as a Feng Shui practitioner. I also blessed it with an affirmation [see Figure 2H]."

Figure 2G: *Maria enhances the Wealth area of her bedroom with an oak jewelry cabinet, an African violet plant, and other Ch'i enhancements.*

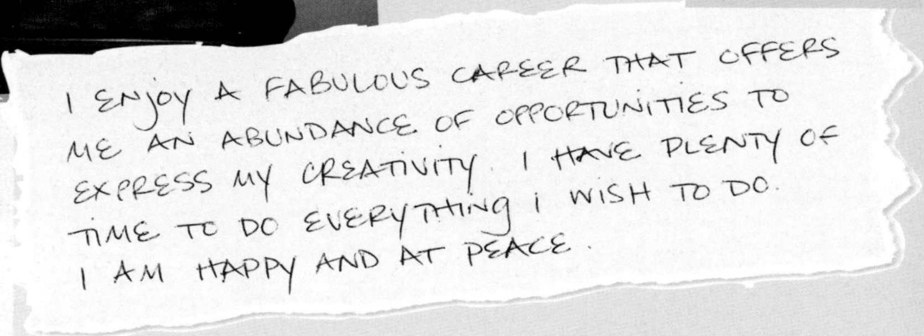

Figure 2H: *Maria's personal affirmation.*

I ENJOY A FABULOUS CAREER THAT OFFERS ME AN ABUNDANCE OF OPPORTUNITIES TO EXPRESS MY CREATIVITY. I HAVE PLENTY OF TIME TO DO EVERYTHING I WISH TO DO. I AM HAPPY AND AT PEACE.

Two days later, Maria met a friend for coffee at a local café. They were sitting at an outdoor table when two of the partners from the firm Maria used to work for walked by.

"We were just talking about you," they told her. "What remarkable timing!"

Maria felt a tingle go through her body. "Well, I was just thinking about calling the firm again to see if you'd changed your mind about hiring part-time employees."

"Call me tomorrow," one of the partners suggested. "We must talk."

Goose bumps—the kind she always got when something good was about to happen—covered Maria's arms. She spent the evening suspended in a delicious sense of being at the right place at the right time. The next day, she called the company.

Maria received an open invitation to return to the firm. "We're expanding into a larger office building and are adding several new associates and partners," she was told. "You can work whatever hours you choose—we'd just love to have you back."

They spent a few more minutes on the phone, and Maria mentioned her Feng Shui practice. "What a coup for us," the partner remarked. "I'd love it if you'd work with the interior designer on our new office and add some Feng Shui inspiration to our new space."

"I was absolutely amazed," Maria recalls. "The law firm door that had been closed had just opened right in front of me; and a Feng Shui door that hadn't even existed before suddenly appeared."

Maria met with the interior designer the next week, and they worked with the plans for the firm's new office. She was also assigned to an attorney who asked her to oversee the design of a new logo and Website for the firm.

"I was thrilled," Maria says today. "It was exactly the kind of project I'd always dreamed of—one that gave me the chance to express my creativity. That night, I looked carefully at the Feng Shui enhancements I'd made: The baker's rack with the fountain and my favorite books in my Career area; my jewelry cabinet and the other treasures I loved in my bedroom and bath; the red fan and candles in the dining room . . . it all seemed to symbolize the celebration of life. I sat there and felt grateful from head to toe for the transformation that was occurring in my life. I could see it happening: One by one, my wishes were coming true."

Postscript: Maria and her husband have recently made another dream come true: They moved from their apartment into a home they purchased. Their new house is near the beach and has a big yard for the family to enjoy.

Summary

To have a child, a happy marriage, and meaningful, creative work are three invaluable treasures in life. As a mom with an engaging career that fulfills her creative expression, Maria truly is a wealthy woman. As she joyfully found out, a door that once appeared to be closed can "blow" open when the Ch'i associated with it is flowing. When Maria focused her attention and intention on creating a meaningful career, an absolute *no* became an absolute *yes,* and to her delight, her entire world changed.

Feng Shui Tips

1. When you wish to improve your employment situation, take steps to enhance these areas in your home and/or workplace: Wealth and Prosperity, Fame and Reputation, Career, and Helpful People and Travel [see Appendix 1]. Be prepared to have doors of opportunity open that were closed before—perhaps even opportunities that are completely different from the ones you expected will present themselves. You could be very pleasantly surprised!

2. Use the associated Bagua colors only if you feel drawn to them. Maria used red objects in her Fame area, blue and purple towels in her Wealth area, and black furniture and decor in her Career area because she liked those colors. If you don't care for the associated colors, there are many other ways to enhance your home and office [see Appendix I].

Maria's Feng Shui Enhancements

❖ Black baker's rack, fountain, and related books in the Career area.

❖ Red fan and candles in the Fame and Reputation area.

❖ Luxurious purple and blue towels in the master bathroom.

❖ A jewelry cabinet, crystal clamshell, blooming plant, and a copy of a check in the Wealth and Prosperity area of the master bedroom.

3

Soap and Mirrors

Every shop owner's dream is to have a successful business that's profitable, and popular in the community. Gary had gone to great lengths to see that his was both. He stocked his gift store with the best in natural cosmetics, bath products, and related books and cards. He had an ideal location that seemed to guarantee success—between a restaurant and a clothing store in a picturesque seaside town. In addition, demographics had shown that this was a town full of people who loved to shop. So how could anyone resist his "scentual" offerings? *Good question,* he thought as he sat in his empty store. Gary knew that there was only one thing left to do. On the advice of his girlfriend, he picked up the phone and booked a Feng Shui consultation with Cynthia Crisp.

Cynthia had been in Gary's store before and had wondered how his business was doing, especially after seeing it through Feng Shui eyes. Her impression was that it was a "yes and no" store. Although Gary sold some wonderful items and many of the product displays were eye-catching and beautiful, others were either chaotic or sparse. This gave shoppers a mixed message that discouraged repeat visits. In addition, Cynthia couldn't help but notice that the area related to Wealth was the least attractive spot in the entire store—plus, that's also where the bathroom was located, and it was a royal mess. Cynthia remembered asking herself why a shop owner would ever let customers use a bathroom that was in such poor shape.

The more Cynthia thought about it, the more excited she felt about having the opportunity to help Gary turn his shop into one big *yes!* After talking with him, she was sure he was just one Feng Shui appointment away from turning his business around.

Cynthia arrived at Gary's store, and he gave her a tour of the space. When they reached the Wealth area [see Figure 3A], he mentioned that no matter what he put there, it just didn't sell.

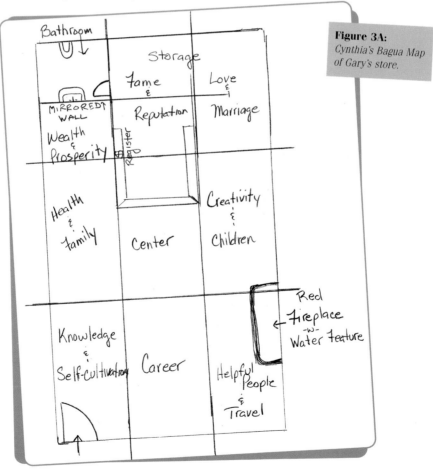

Figure 3A:
Cynthia's Bagua Map of Gary's store.

"I'm not surprised," she said, pointing toward the hideous bathroom. "I remember what's back there, and it's not helping you a bit."

"If you think *that's* bad, wait until you see the storeroom. . . . Promise you won't yell at me!" Gary opened the door slowly to make sure nothing fell on them, clicked on a dim light, and held the door for Cynthia as they stepped into a stuffy room that was in complete chaos.

Cynthia peered at the boxes and supplies that were precariously flung onto high shelves, and asked Gary one simple question: "Do you ever get a headache in here?"

"Are you a psychic, too? Yes, I do."

Cynthia explained. "So many heavy things overhead are headache-makers. Plus, they're dangerous when they're perched up there. And to add insult to possible injury, this area is located behind your cash register and directly relates to your fame and reputation. In other words, the chaos in here prevents your business from becoming successful and well known in the community."

Gary looked a bit pale. "No wonder I'm failing. This is a Feng Shui night-mare!"

Cynthia grinned. "The good news is that you can fix it. Come on, let's start making a list."

They discussed the storeroom and decided that Gary would add more shelving and rearrange the space so that the heavy items were stored on the lower shelves.

The bathroom was next. "It just needs a simple makeover," Cynthia proposed. "Put your cleaning supplies in the storeroom and make it nice in here. Add some photographs or posters that relate to your business—such as women with creamy complexions, fields of lavender, or sumptuous baths. Always think about what it's like to be a customer. What would make this store so pleasing and memorable that you would choose to return here again and again?"

Gary pondered this as they walked back to the front entrance of the store.

Outside, Cynthia asked Gary to take a look at his front window display. He was presented with the same sun-bleached products that shoppers saw as they passed by.

Gesturing toward the window, Cynthia's voice became melodious. "This is where you tantalize your customers with a taste of all the delicious goodies you have waiting inside." Her voice changed. "As it is now, it's certainly not going to whet anyone's appetite."

Gary had to agree. "I get so involved in the store that I forget about the world out there."

They discussed changing the window display as often as once a week to attract shoppers. "Your location and your products are great," Cynthia confirmed. "Now all you need is an irresistible front entrance and an equally irresistible store that people will love to say yes to. The first thing you should do is put planters of lavender and other blooming herbs on either side of the door to welcome your customers. You want to create an alluring atmosphere that's carried throughout the entire space."

Gary kept nodding and taking notes as they walked back inside.

In the Helpful People area of the store, there was a large fireplace that Gary had painted Chinese red. On the mantel was a display of herbal candles, and above that hung a large mirror that was cut into many small squares by a white frame.

"Helpful People relates to your customers. As it stands, the Fire element is too strong, causing people to hurry past this area. You have the Water element represented here by the mirror, but at the moment, it isn't helping you a bit. The images of your customers are being chopped up by all those little squares in the mirror's design. Instead of removing the mirror, I'd suggest that you move the candles and decorate the mantel with items that enhance the Earth and Wood elements [see Appendix II]. For instance, abundant displays of yellow flowers or plants in earthenware pots would eliminate the fractured view customers receive of themselves now. You could also hang a seasonal wreath in front of the mirror to soften it further. Then, put a water feature in front of the fireplace. Your white trim brings in the Metal element, so you're all set there. The goal is to include all five elements in one graceful design so that customers will want to linger in this area." [See Figure 3B.]

Figure 3B: *Gary enhances the Helpful People and Travel area of his store with seasonal mantel decorations, a water feature, and customer seating.*

Enchanted by Cynthia's unique Feng Shui "take" on everything, Gary busily jotted down her suggestions.

Cynthia moved to the Center of the store, where two columns framed a half wall, giving the space some definition. She turned and asked Gary, "Do you like yellow?"

He nodded.

"Good, because that's the perfect color to paint this wall. Yellow represents the Earth element, and it will help to strengthen and ground the store." Cynthia walked back to the area related to Fame and Reputation, where the cash register was located. "I'll be you, and you be the customer," she suggested, getting behind the register. She asked Gary what he saw.

"Not much of anything," he answered, "because I can't see through all the junk on the counter!"

Cynthia waved at Gary and said, "Bingo! And I'm six feet tall and hard to miss!"

They chuckled as Gary sorted through the accumulation of things on the counter and removed three-quarters of it. "*This* is the place for red paint," Cynthia commented, pointing to the shelves behind the cash register. "After you've done that, you should then display something especially appealing on them. Red is related to the Fame area, and it will draw people to the back of the store." [See Figure 3C.]

Gary was happy with the suggestion, knowing that he had left-over red paint in the storeroom.

Cynthia had been saving the best for last. The Wealth area was dark, even in the afternoon light, and it was the sparsest spot in the store. "You're going to love this," she said. "Let's mirror this back wall, floor to ceiling. That will wake this area up and symbolically double your profits. But use one nice big piece of mirror—don't chop it up!"

Gary was all for it. "What should I show off here?"

Cynthia smiled and said, "I bet you already know the answer to that."

"Of course! My most expensive line of products!"

24

Figure 3C: *The area related to Fame is enhanced by a red wall and colorfully packaged gift products.*

Six weeks later, Gary called Cynthia to make a Feng Shui appointment for his house. "So much has happened at the store—it's a whole new world!" He proceeded to give her a detailed account.

Taking Cynthia's suggestions, Gary had painted the wall in the Center of the store a rich, buttery yellow, and the Fame wall bright red. A mirror had been installed in the Wealth area of the store, and shelves had been put up in the storeroom.

"I painted the bathroom a deep pink color and hung two framed luscious lipstick posters. It's a big kiss back there now," Gary proudly told Cynthia. "Customers ask to use the bathroom and then ask for some of that lipstick. I've also been changing the window display about once a week. It's easier to remember now that I have to water the pots of lavender by the door. And, your Feng Shui enthusiasm is contagious, Cynthia. I did something you didn't even ask me to do: I put two 'helpful people' reading chairs by the books near the fireplace. I also made a water feature out of the same kind of pot I planted the lavender in and did a whole seasonal display across the mantel. See, I remembered what you said about a theme."

Cynthia was impressed. Gary sounded like a different man from the one she'd worked with not so long ago.

"And business . . . well, first of all, the Wealth area is king. As soon as I put product out there, it's sold. Actually, everything's selling really well, and customers are in here all day long. An interior designer came in and raved about the place—I gave her your card.

"And to top it all off, a man offered to buy the entire store—lock, stock, and barrel—for his wife. Can you believe it? He was totally serious. I told him that I've just gotten this place rolling and I'm having too much fun . . . but if his wife wanted to help me open my second store, well, I'm interested."

Summary

Gary's story is a good example of a business that carried a mixed message: (1) It was in a *yes* location, (2) said *no* in the front window, (3) conveyed a combination of *yes* and *no* throughout the store, and (4) loudly expressed *no* in the storeroom and bathroom. Businesses with this type of problem tend to repeatedly lurch forward a little and then screech to a halt, much like driving with the brake and the accelerator on at the same time. As Cynthia demonstrated, the trick is to identify the *nos* and transform them into *yeses,* so that customers have a consistently harmonious shopping experience that entices them to return.

The same pattern can also take place in a home. For instance, the living room may be a *yes,* the kitchen a *no,* the bedroom a *yes,* and the bathroom and storage areas a *no.* The most successful businesses—and the most comfortable homes—are affirmational throughout, meaning that they are one big *yes!*

Feng Shui Tips

1. Take a Feng Shui survey of the *yeses* and *nos* in your home and business. If any area or item irritates, overwhelms, or confuses you, it's a *no*. Follow these practical guidelines to achieve your goal:

- surround yourself with things that make a positive impression on you;
- focus on comfort and safety to achieve a beautiful result; and
- keep places and things simplified and organized.

Whatever you need to do to turn a *no* into a *yes* will be well worth it.

2. Clear, bright mirrors reflect clear, bright Ch'i. Avoid mirrors designed to break up or distort an image, such as those made up of many beveled pieces or small squares, for they distort Ch'i flow. Hang mirrors so that they reflect at least the entire head, with several inches to spare.

Gary's Feng Shui Enhancements

- Plants to adorn the front entrance.
- Window displays changed weekly.
- A balance of the five elements, and camouflaging and softening the mirror in the Helpful People and Travel area.
- A yellow wall to strengthen the Center of the store.
- A red wall in the Fame area.
- Clearing the clutter on the cash register counter.
- A mirrored wall in the Prosperity area.
- Bathroom and storeroom improvements.

4

Door Number One

After years of working for other people, Peter and Carol had finally reached their goal: They were both self-employed and worked out of their home. Peter's photography business was located in a large room that was originally the den, which provided enough space for a darkroom as well as an office. Carol, a freelance journalist, had decided to put her office in an extra bedroom. It had seemed like the ideal plan . . . until they actually tried it.

In no time, the dark side of home-based businesses became quite apparent to both Peter and Carol. For instance, they discovered the challenge of separating business from home life: Carol found herself spending most of the day in her robe, distracted by the never-ending cycle of domestic chores; and because Peter's business was constantly "in his face," he couldn't seem to relax. He often worked on his projects until late at night, leaving Carol to spend evenings alone in the next room.

Tension built between the couple, especially when both of their businesses took a nosedive. Carol was alarmed—their brilliant plan wasn't working, and if they didn't do something fast, they'd be forced to rejoin the rat race.

Carol thought of Lainie Wrightson, a Feng Shui practitioner she'd written about for a local newspaper. Maybe Lainie would be able to shed some light on their situation. It was certainly worth a try. Carol picked up the phone and made an appointment.

When Lainie pulled up in front of the house, she was confused. Where was the front entrance? She approached the house slowly, looking for clues as to which door to use—there were two of them, and neither seemed inviting. She picked the door closest to the driveway and knocked. A voice from the other side of the door instructed her to go to the next one, where Carol and Peter greeted her.

"Did you have any problem finding us?" Carol asked.

"I found the house easily, but your front door. . . . Do you have many people visiting you here?"

"Well, some," Peter said. "We don't use the door you tried first—even though it's supposedly the front entrance—because this door is closer to the garage. Everyone gets confused when they come here for the first time."

Lainie decided to jump right in. "Well, I have to tell you, the Ch'i gets confused, too. In Feng Shui, we call the front door the 'mouth of Ch'i,' through which energy, like oxygen, enters the home. To attract success and prosperity to your door, we make sure your front entrance is clearly marked and very welcoming."

Carol looked at Peter. "Uh-oh, we're already in trouble. Wait 'til Lainie sees what's *behind* the front door."

They went around to the foyer by the front entrance. Instead of a welcoming entryway, Lainie saw a storeroom. Boxes of photo supplies and equipment were haphazardly stacked against the door and walls, and other things had found their way into the space as well—Lainie noticed sports equipment and boxes marked "memorabilia."

Peter turned to Lainie and asked, "What's wrong with this? I know where almost everything is."

Lainie exchanged a glance with Carol. "I'm sure you do, Peter. But this area is directly related to your career [see Figure 4A], and needs to be opened up so that new life can flow into your business. As it is now, my guess is that it's suffocating."

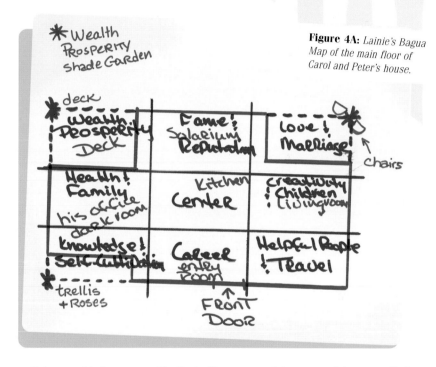

Figure 4A: *Lainie's Bagua Map of the main floor of Carol and Peter's house.*

Peter couldn't argue with that. "I suppose this means I have to find other places for all this stuff," he sighed. "Are you going to help me figure that out?"

Lainie promised that she would, and the three of them toured the rest of the main floor of the house. Lainie quickly ascertained that the Wealth and Love areas were missing [see Figure 4A], as was a portion of the Knowledge area. "You guys have actually done very well, considering the structure of your house. But just out of curiosity, have either of you noticed a strain in your relationship?"

Carol rolled her eyes. "Oh, no, we haven't tried to kill each other in at least a week, have we, honey?"

They all laughed. "This is like therapy," Peter said. "How did you know to ask that question?"

"Because the shape of your house excludes the area related to love relationships," Lainie explained, "which means that there's no structure to support marital happiness. It also excludes the areas associated with prosperity and knowledge. But let me say that this can all become a thing of the past, because I'm going to show you how to correct it." Lainie saw the distress on their faces turn to relief. She continued, "We'll sit down and figure it all out as soon as I see the upstairs."

The second floor revealed the reasons for Carol's inability to focus on work. The desk in her little office was placed so that she had no view of the door, and her computer was in the bedroom.

"Why do you have your computer in the bedroom?" Lainie wondered.

"I moved it in there because I can't seem to concentrate in my office. Of course, writing in the bedroom makes me sleepy, so that's not working either. What do you suggest?"

Lainie thought for a moment. "I think that you should arrange your office so that it works well for *you*. First, let's move your desk to give you a view of the door. If you want, it can be situated so that you have a peripheral view of both the window and the door. Sit in your chair and roll around until you find the right spot."

Carol rolled her chair into several areas of the room. On the third try, she exclaimed, "This feels good right here, and I have a view of everything. What a difference this makes!"

Peter brought in the computer from the bedroom, and within minutes, Carol's office was ready to go. She was thrilled and gave her husband a big hug.

"Your closet's in the Wealth area of this room," Lainie pointed out. "Is it neat in there?"

"Unlike other people we know," Carol said smugly, casting a look in Peter's direction, "*my* storage area is quite organized." She opened the door to reveal shelves neatly arranged with office supplies and a row of matching filing cabinets.

"Well, Peter, you certainly have the right partner to help you get things sorted out downstairs," Lainie remarked. "I recommend that each of you also organize your *thoughts*. Write down an affirmation related to your work and post it in both of your offices, something like: *'My work as a photographer—or freelance writer—is plentiful, enjoyable, and profitable.'*"

They moved into the master bedroom, where Lainie proposed that they add a love seat or two comfortable reading chairs where Carol's computer had previously been stationed. "It will enhance the spirit of romance in your bedroom and energize the Love and Marriage area in here."

They returned downstairs to talk about arranging Peter's things and enhancing the missing Wealth, Love, and Knowledge areas. Lainie observed that along the way, something had changed between Peter and Carol. They were now working seamlessly together, generating one brilliant idea after another. *They're going to be fine,* Lainie thought, as she listened to them build upon each other's ideas. *They've got the information and the enthusiasm they need to put their lives back on track.*

About a month later, Lainie called the couple to find out how things were progressing.

Carol excitedly gave her the scoop. "We've been Feng Shui maniacs! The first thing we did was dig out the foyer and open up our front entrance. I can't tell you what a difference it's made. Peter's stuff is now neatly stored in several places—including in his office closet, which was a mess until I got my hands on it. Boy, has he changed! It's been like a second honeymoon around here.

"Anyway, we put planters shaped like rabbits on either side of the front entrance and trimmed back the plants along the pathway [see Figure 4B]. As soon as we did that, Peter's aunt called and offered to give us an heirloom chest and mirror that he's always loved. So we put them in the foyer [see Figure 4C] to enhance the Career area, and let me tell you, it worked. He's gotten more wedding contracts in the last couple of weeks than he has in an entire year! In fact, so much is happening that it almost scared us. But then I started helping him with the phones and scheduling, and I'm enjoying that much more than writing. We make a great team. We also adopted the affirmation you suggested as an example, but modified it a bit [see Figure 4D]."

Figure 4B: *Carol and Peter's front entrance is easy to approach and is now embellished with planters and a welcome mat.*

Our work is plentiful, enjoyable, and profitable. We are happy, healthy, and prosperous!

Figure 4D: *Carol and Peter's personal affirmation.*

Figure 4C: *Foyer enhancements include an heirloom chest and mirror, statuary, a lamp, and a favorite photo.*

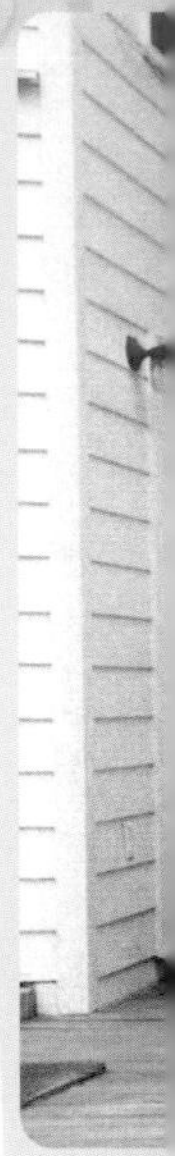

Lainie listened intently. From what Carol was saying, it sounded as if they must have also enhanced their Love and Marriage area. "So did you and Peter do anything out back?"

"We sure did! We put two Adirondack chairs in our Love area [see Figure 4E], and we sit out there with our coffee in the mornings. I made an outdoor garden room in the Wealth area [see Figure 4F], and that's our evening place. Remember how there was no furniture out there? Well, now there's a table, chairs, an umbrella, and tons of flowers in ceramic pots. I figured we had to make it very rich looking, so there's not a plastic pot in the bunch." Carol took a breath and continued on. "Oh, and we put up a trellis and planted climbing roses to anchor the Knowledge area in the front yard. You know, Lainie, I never knew I liked gardening so much," Carol chuckled. "If we're this busy already, I wonder what will happen to our business when I enhance the Wealth area of the property. That's next on my list."

Lainie told Carol how happy she was for her and Peter, and asked that they keep her posted.

Figure 4E: *Carol and Peter enhanced their Love and Marriage area with two outdoor chairs, a table, and a plant.*

Figure 4F: *The backyard deck becomes a Wealth-related oasis.*

37

About six weeks later, Carol called Lainie to update her on two things that she'd done since she last talked to her. Carol had cleared the brush away from the wooded Wealth area of their yard and planted a shade garden [see Figure 4G].

In addition, Carol had expanded the menu of choices that Peter's photography business offered. The day she completed the shade garden, a customer called to schedule the most expensive package their business could provide for her daughter's wedding. No, a deposit wasn't going to be necessary—this customer wished to pay in full, now.

"I had to call and tell you!" The joy in Carol's voice was infectious. "Peter has so much work pouring in that he asked me to see if you knew any way to slow it down! I told him we'd hire another photographer, for goodness' sake. This is our opportunity to share the wealth."

Figure 4G: *A statue and flowers highlight the shade garden Carol planted in the Wealth area of the property.*

Postscript: Carol's love for gardening has led her to tackle the entire yard, turning it into a woodland paradise. She and Peter are remodeling the detached garage to house his photography business, and they're building a small studio for her so that they can move both of their businesses out of the house. Peter has also developed a passion for yoga and is becoming a yoga teacher. Carol and Peter are living the life of their intention—one filled with health, happiness, and prosperity.

Summary

Peter and Carol had unknowingly dammed the vital flow of energy from entering their home when they blocked off their front door. Deprived of the constant nourishment that the mouth of Ch'i provides, their happiness and success languished. We witness this in nature when debris collects and dams a river—the water becomes too still and stagnates, which is exactly what occurred energetically in Peter and Carol's home. When they removed the debris and opened up the front entrance, the flow of Ch'i, like water, naturally returned. They also benefited from defining the Bagua areas located outdoors to contain the energy of prosperity, intimacy, and wisdom, much like the banks that define and contain a river.

Feng Shui Tip

Welcome auspicious people, experiences, and opportunities into your life by making your front entrance "entrancing" and easy to find. Embellish it with pleasant lighting, flowers, statuary, seating, and other enhancements that say *welcome*. Whether it's a magnificent fountain or a simple wreath on the door, treat your home's mouth of Ch'i with special care. In addition, dedicate your bedroom to rest, rejuvenation, and romance. Locate items that speak of activity—such as computers and exercise equipment—in other rooms.

Peter and Carol's Feng Shui Enhancements

- Opening up and beautifying the front entrance to their house.
- Enhancing the foyer with an heirloom chest, mirror, and other decor.
- Removing the computer from the bedroom.
- Rearranging Carol's office to gain a view of the door.
- Creating an outdoor garden room to complete the Wealth area of the house, and planting a shade garden to enhance the Wealth area of the property.
- Placing two Adirondack chairs and a table to define the Love area of the yard.
- Adding a trellis and roses to the Knowledge area of the house.

5

Wind, Water, and Wealth

As an interior designer, Judy Lonn already had a talent for decorating homes and offices. So when a magazine article on Feng Shui caught her attention, she decided to find out more about it. She purchased a Feng Shui audio program to listen to on a road trip she was taking, and by the time she returned, she knew that this was information she'd intuitively understood and practiced her entire life.

Judy attended a local Feng Shui workshop and learned how to apply the Bagua Map [see Appendix I] to her house. The results were startling. She discovered that the structure of the coastal home she shared with her husband and two daughters left the Wealth and Prosperity area out in the breeze—or a strong ocean wind to be exact [see Figure 5A]. No wonder she had financial troubles!

Looking at her Bagua Map again, Judy saw that the area related to her family's finances was in a windswept part of the backyard, mirroring the fact that their money was continually being "swept away" by unexpected expenses. With no structure to hold their wealth in place, this family was paying more for their coastal location than they realized.

"I had to do something immediately," Judy recalls. "So I hung a wind chime to call in the Ch'i of prosperity [see Figure 5B] and dragged a few large potted palms over to define the Wealth area [see Figure 5C]."

41

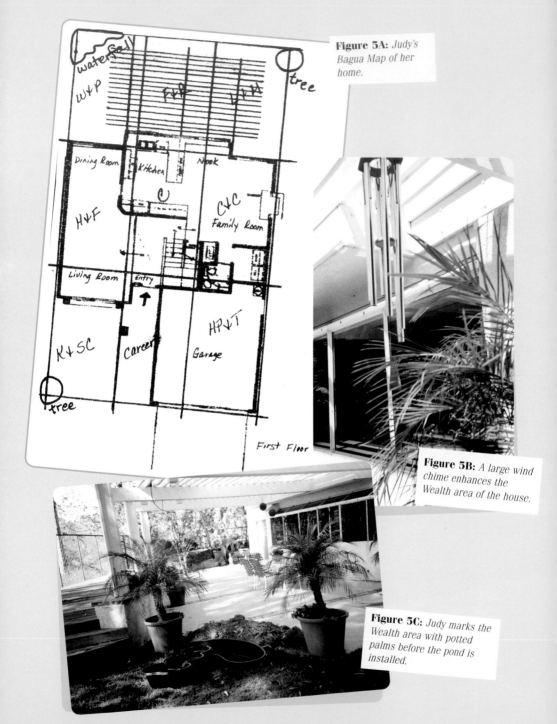

Figure 5A: *Judy's Bagua Map of her home.*

Figure 5B: *A large wind chime enhances the Wealth area of the house.*

Figure 5C: *Judy marks the Wealth area with potted palms before the pond is installed.*

Soon after, Judy mentioned to her brother that she'd be attending Feng Shui practitioner training when she had the funds to do so. Two days later, she received a big surprise: Her father, who had rarely given Judy money for any reason, offered to pay for her training.

"My brother had spoken with Dad, and he decided to pay my tuition. It was so out of character that I thought he was kidding," Judy remembers. "But Dad said he was happy to do it."

Now Feng Shui really had Judy's attention. She enrolled in the next practitioner training and returned home ready to try her Feng Shui hand on the inside of her own house.

"I decided to focus on prosperity," Judy says, "so I took two fancy envelopes and put a personal check for $5,000 into each one, along with a written affirmation. It read: *'I am open and ready to receive wealth and prosperity in my life.'*"

Judy then placed one envelope in the Wealth area of her family room and the other in the Wealth area of her kitchen [see Figure 5D]. Three weeks later, her father called to say he'd sent her something special by registered mail. The next day she received her dad's package, which contained a note about his wish to share some of his investment profits with her . . . and a check for $10,000.

Figure 5D: *A decorative red envelope holding an affirmational check and other personally chosen enhancements brighten the Wealth areas of the kitchen and family room.*

Feng Shui was now starting to get Russ, Judy's husband, to sit up and take notice. Suddenly, he was more than happy to help her with a more ambitious project in the Wealth and Prosperity area outside. Judy and Russ installed a pond and waterfall that flowed toward the house, symbolizing the Ch'i of prosperity flowing into their home [see Figure 5E].

Figure 5E: *Judy's pond and waterfall symbolize prosperity constantly flowing into the house.*

Figure 5F: *Judy and her daughters enjoy their backyard oasis.*

"The day we turned on the waterfall, we received a refund check from the IRS that we'd been expecting—for more than three years," Judy says today. "And we weren't even finished with our project!"

Russ and Judy went on to add sculptural rocks and underwater lights to the waterfall, making it into an outdoor sanctuary that symbolizes plentiful finances.

Judy turned her Feng Shui attention indoors again. She knew that a home's clutter blocks good fortune from entering, so she decided to take a good look around. What she found didn't fall into the traditional classification of *clutter*, but Judy did discover many things that hadn't been used in a long time and probably never would be. Back in the recesses of the kitchen and bathroom cabinets, linen closet, and other storage areas was a plethora of unused belongings that did nothing more than take up space.

"I packed them all up for the neighborhood garage sale. I got rid of a ton of stuff—kitchen gadgets, old sheets and towels, baby toys and clothes, and additional odds and ends that other people would love." Judy smiles at the memory of it now. "And at the last minute, I threw in the old weather-beaten patio furniture that had been sitting out in our Wealth area. What we made from that garage sale was enough to buy a new patio set."

With the backyard looking more beautifully "Feng Shuied" than ever [see Figure 5F], Judy wondered what was coming next.

Her answer arrived one evening when a woman from a refinancing company called. Although Judy and Russ had always been turned down for these offers in the past, Judy found that this call went much differently.

"Given the fortunate blessings of the recent past, I don't know why I was surprised that we actually qualified to refinance our house," Judy recollects. "We never had before . . . but this time we did. The refinance has enabled us to pull some equity out of the house that gives me the resources to make a personal dream come true. After 15 years of not having a dedicated space in the house for a computer, I'm remodeling the alcove in the upstairs hall to be the family computer station. After it's complete, my next goal is to enhance the Helpful People and Travel area, which happens to be in the garage. After that, we want to install windscreens around the back patio so that we can entertain out there all year long.

"That's the beauty and the richness of life," Judy cheerfully explains. "There's always more!"

Postscript: Two weeks after Judy enhanced the garage (their home's Helpful People and Travel area) with wall hangings depicting angels, her uncle invited the entire family to join him on a Caribbean cruise, all expenses paid.

Summary

Judy produced excellent results with her Feng Shui work, stemming from her expertise in blending the "wind Ch'i" of clear intentions with the "water Ch'i" of environmental enhancements. This is a skill anyone can develop—and the more you practice setting your intentions with clarity and purpose, the better you become at manifesting good fortune in your life.

Feng Shui Tips

1. Use affirmations, prayers, and other powerful symbols to hold your goals and wishes in place. Judy's use of prosperity affirmations is one example.

2. Simplify and organize your storage areas. You'll attract positive people, places, and things into your life by letting go of the old to make room for the new.

Judy's Feng Shui Enhancements

- ⬧ Adding palms, wind chimes, a pond, a waterfall, rocks, and lighting to the outdoor Wealth and Prosperity area.

- ⬧ Placing prosperity affirmations in red envelopes in two indoor Wealth and Prosperity areas.

- ⬧ Identifying and letting go of unneeded possessions.

6

All Spruced Up

Now that her daughter was six months old, Anna was ready to go back to work as a real-estate agent, yet none of her attempts to reenter the field seemed to be paying off very well. She found herself wondering if perhaps Feng Shui might be able to help.

Anna called practitioner BJ Gorman and asked her just one question: "Can Feng Shui do anything about feeling stuck?"

BJ said she'd see what she could do.

BJ spotted the first Feng Shui challenge as soon as she pulled up to Anna's house. As she parked her car, BJ noticed that the house was mostly hidden behind four gigantic blue spruce trees in the front yard [see Figure 6A]. As beautiful as they were, the trees' thick boughs prevented Ch'i from flowing easily to the house. *No wonder Anna is "opportunity challenged,"* BJ thought.

Figure 6A: *The front view of Anna's home.*

Once BJ got inside, she observed that Anna's living room had two large picture windows, but all she could see out of them were masses of blue branches. In addition, a large dog cage and two oversized marble end tables dominated the room. [See Figure 6B.]

"Anna, I can see that your feelings of being stuck originate right here," BJ said, looking around the room. "We're standing in the area related to careers [see Figure 6C], and a giant cage and two very heavy tables hold the 'I'm stuck' experience in place. I'd highly recommend that you let these things go! You also need to prune the bottom branches of those spruces so that light and energy can flow into this room. The next thing you know, your career will take off, and you'll be so busy that you'll be giving work away."

Figure 6B: *Anna's living room is darkened by the large trees, and crowded by the heavy marble tables.*

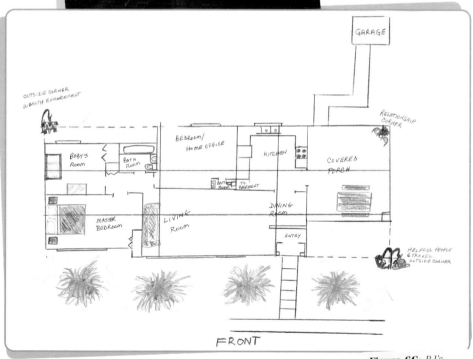

Figure 6C: *BJ's Bagua Map of Anna's house.*

49

Anna agreed. Seeing her living room through new eyes, she realized that what BJ said was true—the space *was* dark and crowded. "No wonder I've been feeling so gloomy. And speaking of gloomy, wait until you see my office."

Anna led BJ down to a dank little space in the basement. "I set this up when I got pregnant and decided to work from home," she explained. "But I hate it down here."

BJ could certainly understand why. Anna's desk was jammed into a dark corner with computer equipment and papers heaped on top of it. In order for Anna to sit at her desk, she had to have her back to an immense recreation room. This was where her husband, Tony, and two stepsons watched TV when the boys were visiting—it was a perfect boys' hangout room, not a home office.

When BJ discovered that the boys, who preferred to sleep downstairs, had a bedroom on the main floor, a lightbulb went on in her head. "Let's put the boys' bedroom furniture down here and move your office upstairs! You'll think you're in heaven when you have a work space with natural light and some privacy."

Anna smiled. Just the thought of it made her feel better.

Continuing on throughout the house and yard, BJ noticed a theme emerging—clutter. But before she could say anything, Anna volunteered an explanation: "Since my pregnancy, the house has become very disorganized. I used to be able to stay on top of it, but Tony's a pack rat, and it's just gotten out of control."

BJ explained Feng Shui's perspective on this subject. "Clutter depletes the vitality of *every* part of your life, including your career. Simply put, all of this stuff is preventing the blessings of prosperity from flowing your way. It's crucial for you to sort through the piles and let go of whatever is no longer useful."

Together, BJ and Anna looked at the Bagua Map of the house [see Figure 6C]. The Love and Marriage area was located in an unfurnished back porch, while the house's shape left the Wealth and Prosperity and the Helpful People and Travel areas out in the yard. BJ suggested that the two missing areas be anchored by placing meaningful objects at the corners. She also urged Anna to embellish the "Love" porch, and arrange several beautiful objects near the front door to act as "greeters." For although the two women joked about how perfect the house would be for a poor, single hermit, this was hardly how Anna wanted to live her life.

As soon as BJ left, Anna began to get to work. She thought about what BJ had said about anchors for Wealth and Helpful People, so she rooted around in her stuff, and found two shepherd's crooks to do the job. Anna used one of them, which held a Star of David wind chime, to secure the Wealth corner [see Figure 6D]; then she placed a bird feeder on the other and put it in the Helpful People area.

Anna continued by decorating the porch with plants and patio furniture, putting a large pot of flowers on the front step, calling a tree-trimming company, and listing "two marble block tables and one large dog cage" in the local newspaper.

Figure 6D: *Anna chose a shepherd's crook, embellished with a Star of David wind chime, to mark the Wealth and Prosperity area of the house.*

Now it was time to attack the clutter. What a job! Anna realized that not only was there junk in every room, it was piled all around the outside of the house as well. Tony immediately took offense when she told him this, and he told her to keep her "busy little hands" to herself—he didn't want her going through any of his things. Anna called BJ for direction.

"You have plenty to do just getting your own stuff organized," BJ counseled. "But I bet that by the time you're done, he'll be begging you to help him with his junk!"

Anna returned to her own tasks. Much to the delight of her stepsons, their beds were moved downstairs, and she set up a comfortable private office upstairs. As soon as she plugged in the phone, she received a call asking if she could help a couple to purchase a home in the area. Anna said that she absolutely could.

Three weeks later, the trees were pruned [see Figure 6E], the dog cage and marble tables were sold, and a charity had received many carloads of items from Anna's house. And now, when visitors arrived, they were greeted by one of Anna and Tony's favorite pieces of art and a porcelain lamp they absolutely loved in the entryway [see Figure 6F].

Life quickly began to show signs of improvement: The bank notified Anna and Tony that they'd been overpaying on their mortgage, sent them a refund, and lowered their monthly payments. Then Tony's employers suddenly offered to pay for him to take a series of classes that would prepare him for a promotion in the company. Tony had asked that he be permitted to attend these classes many times before, but had been unsuccessful. It seemed to him that this opportunity had come "right out of the blue."

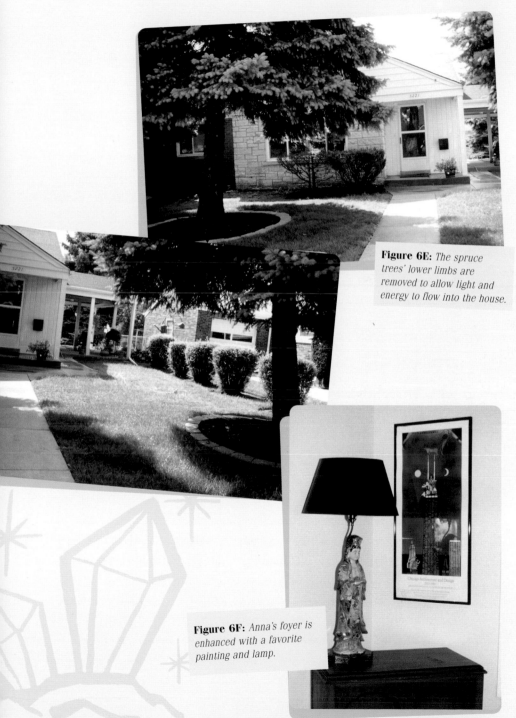

Figure 6E: *The spruce trees' lower limbs are removed to allow light and energy to flow into the house.*

Figure 6F: *Anna's foyer is enhanced with a favorite painting and lamp.*

Anna, Tony, and the kids also took their first family trip—something Tony said he'd never do—and had a great time. Soon after, Anna and Tony went on the first romantic getaway of their marriage. Now they're planning a family vacation to California.

"I'm still pinching myself about this one," Anna told BJ recently. "Tony used to absolutely refuse to travel. Now he actually looks forward to it."

BJ asked Anna if she'd noticed any other changes. "As a matter of fact, yes," Anna answered. "For the first time since we've lived here, we're getting to know several of our neighbors. They began to drop by after the trees were trimmed and I spruced up our 'love porch,' as you call it. They're also interested in the real estate around here, so I get a lot of referrals from them. And we hosted the first big party that anyone in the family had had in years. Simply put, we've become more social!"

All of this change culminated in Anna and Tony selling their "blue spruce house" and purchasing a bigger home that better suits their family's needs. Anna now leads sales trainings for real-estate agents at a large firm, which is a lucrative position with flexible hours that gives her plenty of time with her family. And true to BJ's prediction, Tony finally *did* ask Anna to help him sort through his personal domain of clutter, 90 percent of which was sold at their local humane society's summer garage sale.

Summary

Multiple blockages prevented the Ch'i of happiness and success from entering Anna's home. Her experience of being stuck in life was held in place by the overbearing trees, heavy marble tables, large cage, piles of clutter, and depressing basement office. In addition, the structure of the house left the Wealth, Love, and Helpful People areas unsupported.

It's interesting that after Anna and Tony "lifted" the trees, eliminated their clutter, moved Anna's office upstairs, and enhanced their Wealth, Love, Helpful People, and Career areas, their financial, social, and marital happiness increased accordingly. Anna and Tony's home became a place where the vital energy of happiness and prosperity could reside. In addition, Tony eventually became willing to do his part after he experienced the difference Anna's Feng Shui enhancements made in their lives.

Feng Shui Tips

1. Plant trees far enough away from the house so that they don't block the flow of Ch'i. Before actually removing trees that are too close, consider pruning or lacing them. This will control root growth and will allow light and Ch'i to pass through.

2. Locate a home office in a place that provides natural light and some peace and quiet. If necessary, rearrange the house, as Anna did, to best suit your needs.

3. Oftentimes, you'll already have lovely things that can be used to improve Ch'i flow. For instance, Anna had the shepherd's crooks and foyer enhancements right there in her house. Look around for things you already own before buying new ones. Be creative and inventive, and enjoy the process of improving the vitality of your home by putting all the right things in all the right places.

Anna's Feng Shui Enhancements

- ⊕ Placing a shepherd's crook in the Wealth and Helpful People areas outdoors.

- ⊕ Trimming the trees.

- ⊕ Removing clutter.

- ⊕ Making the porch related to Love and Marriage an enjoyable place to spend time.

- ⊕ Putting plants and flowers on the porch and front steps.

- ⊕ Enhancing the foyer with a special painting and lamp.

- ⊕ Moving the home office from the basement to an upstairs bedroom.

Patented Glory

There are many glamorous businesses in the world, but most people would agree that pest control isn't one of them—oftentimes, even Dory thought it was odd that she loved this profession so much. But she was fascinated by the world of bugs, especially by how tenacious and ultimately unstoppable they were.

Dory's quest for natural deterrents to insects had led to the invention of a nontoxic alternative to chemical pesticides that effectively eliminated the whitefly. Her goal was to have her "gold dust" patented so that she could manufacture and distribute it to nurseries and garden-supply wholesalers. Yet after three years of lawyers and complications, she still didn't have her patent.

When Dory heard Ellen Schneider speak on Feng Shui at a Women in Business meeting, she decided a consultation was exactly what she needed. She called Ellen immediately and made an appointment.

Ellen toured Dory's facility and was struck by one prevailing problem—the place was filthy, inside and out. A mud-splattered stucco wall encircled the front of the building, and between the wall and the front entrance was a pond full of green scum. Outside the building were piles of old machinery, canisters, and dead plants; inside, the offices and store-room were dusty and cluttered. Dory agreed that the place was a mess, but she'd never seen any reason to keep it tidy since business was done off-premises and no customers ever came into the place. Ellen had witnessed this in other businesses that didn't deal directly with the public, and she told Dory how impractical that theory was.

"Dory, *you and your employees* are here," Ellen said. "And you're all very important because you're running the business. Everything—the swampy pond, the piles of refuse, the overflowing trash cans, the dirty bathroom—is talking to you all the time."

Dory shook her head. "That's a scary thought. If this junk is talking to me, it has nothing nice to say."

Ellen agreed. "You're going to be very pleasantly surprised to see what happens to your business when you clear away all of the debris from in and around the building."

Dory then took Ellen to the small work areas of the company's six employees. Ellen looked carefully at the placement of each desk and suggested that several of them be moved to gain a view of the door. And once again, Ellen found that clutter ruled every area, which prompted a discussion about buying more filing cabinets and shelves.

"Fran, my secretary, has been asking for more storage for ages," Dory confessed. "I've just never made it a priority."

Ellen assured her that it would make a big difference. She went on to point out that, throughout the building, there was a decided lack of art. Besides the occasional bug-of-the-month gift calendar swinging from a thumbtack, nothing relieved the vast expanse of white space on the walls.

"Let's give your employees something wonderful to look at throughout the day. Something inspiring, like—"

Before Ellen could finish her sentence, Dory interrupted. "Like flowers—big, colorful posters of flowers! We have a whole pile of them somewhere." They both looked at the heaps of stuff everywhere and laughed. "Fran will find them," Dory promised.

The tour revealed another Feng Shui challenge that changed the way Ellen applied the Bagua Map to the building [see Figure 7A]. "This is very interesting," she told Dory. "The roof that protects the picnic table out back changes the flow of Ch'i and effectively places your Wealth and Fame areas out in the dirt. With no structure to contain those two areas, I can see why it's been very difficult to manifest a powerful symbol of both fame and wealth—such as a patent."

Figure 7A: *Ellen's Bagua Map of Dory's business.*

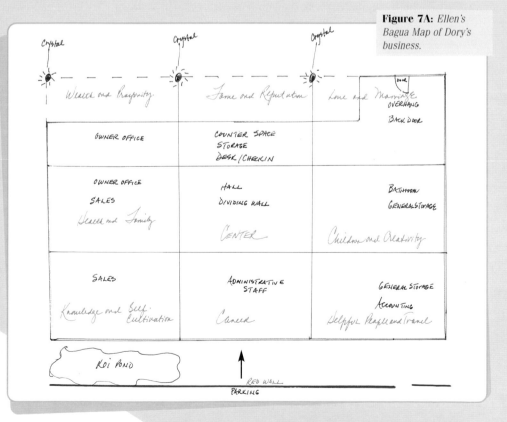

Dory looked troubled. "That roof covers the break area for my employees and protects them from the midday sun."

Ellen assured her that enhancements could be made that didn't entail removing the roof. "We'll get back to that later," she said. "Now, what about that signage out front? It looks like it's been there for a while."

Dory conceded that it was quite dated and advertised services they no longer offered. "I'll be the first to admit that it needs to be changed."

Ellen concurred. "And while you're at it, make that mud fence of a wall into a delightful landmark. All it will take is a few buckets of red paint."

A week later, Dory received Ellen's written report. It began with this statement: "Businesses are entities that are alive and teeming with customers, employees, and vendors who are the sources of your revenue, inspiration, technology, and products. The more safe, comfortable, and beautiful your environment, the more productive and successful your business will become. Your physical surroundings reinforce your values and vision."

Ellen's suggestions for Dory were as follows:

1. *Draw attention to the business and provide a new landmark in the community by painting the front wall a bright color, such as red. Choose a symbol or logo that positively reflects your business and incorporate it into your signage and advertising.*

2. To strengthen your Wealth and Fame areas, purchase three natural quartz crystals, approximately three inches in length. Bury them, points up, in the three areas marked on the enclosed Bagua Map [see Figure 7A].

3. To attract auspicious opportunities to your door, enhance the entrance area by cleaning and maintaining the pond. Add fish, water plants, and other appropriate embellishments. Pots of flowers, such as red geraniums, on either side of the front entrance are also recommended.

4. Remove all trash from outside and inside the building. Avoid keeping items that are broken or unusable for any reason. Paint window trim and other weathered areas. Keep all windows clean.

5. Schedule a professional service to deep-clean the office, and then have them return a minimum of every other week.

6. *The storeroom needs heavy-duty industrial shelving and general organization. Because you're storing chemicals, be sure that the ventilation fan is always working.*

7. *Rearrange desks, add cabinets and shelves as needed, and add art, as we discussed.*

Dory implemented all of Ellen's suggestions over the next few months [see Figure 7B]. The wall was painted red, the pond went from alarming to alluring, and professional cleaners and shelving installers came and went. Dory chose the red hibiscus flower as her business logo, hung hibiscus banners on either side of the front entrance, and had new signage installed. Following Ellen's "treasure map," Dory envisioned the prized patent in her hand and dutifully buried the quartz crystals to anchor Fame and Prosperity. Dory's employees organized their space, adding cabinets and shelves as needed. Fran did indeed find the flower posters, and everyone chose their favorites for framing.

Dory noticed an immediate improvement in business—in fact, she exceeded her financial goals for the quarter—and in her attitude. Little had she realized how much stress she'd felt in the past, but being at work had turned from painful to enjoyable. Her employees clearly felt the same way: The whining and complaining she'd endured was replaced with steady productivity. All of this was wonderful, but for Dory, the best result was that shortly after completing her Feng Shui assignments, she was awarded her patent.

Figure 7B: *Dory's business after making Feng Shui enhancements.*

Summary

There's a pervasive belief in our culture that certain trash or clutter just doesn't matter. In this case, Dory believed that because customers didn't visit her place of business, it didn't matter how dirty and chaotic it was. Ellen helped her realize that it was crucial to her success to act as if the building did have a steady stream of visitors—because, in fact, it did, in the form of Dory and her employees. Safety, comfort, and beauty *always* matter. Improving Dory's physical surroundings provided her with a powerful "before-and-after" experience of watching her employees move from peevish mediocrity to empowered productivity. The act of burying the crystals was a symbolic enhancement—an active prayer—that served to hold her heart's desire in place. Now, every time Dory looks out at the back of the property, she remembers the moment she planted the crystals into the earth and what they stand for. And so, we see it again . . . the wind and the water—the goal and the action—harmoniously coupled to create positive change.

Feng Shui Tip

The spirit of any business is enlivened by art and decor that accurately reflects the purpose of that business. In Dory's case, the hibiscus flower logo and posters of flowers throughout her facility aesthetically represent the essence of her company. Increase *your* success by selecting a theme and employing inspirational imagery that reflects the essence of your business. Themes can be artfully integrated with the Bagua enhancements as well—for instance, in Dory's case, posters featuring purple or red flowers were placed in the Wealth area, while whimsical, playful images of flowers were picked to highlight the Children and Creativity area.

Dory's Feng Shui Enhancements

- Removing trash and clutter.

- Restoring the pond.

- Finding a new logo and art that represented the theme of the business.

- Organizing each work station.

- Making a red "landmark" wall.

- Placing banners and flowers on the front entrance.

- Burying natural quartz crystals to symbolically enhance the Wealth and Fame areas.

8

Out with the Old, In with the New

Joe had a big problem: He was tired all the time and any little issue stressed him out—which was a serious predicament since he was a high-school teacher and dealt with classrooms filled with teenagers all week long. Medical tests showed that he was healthy, so why did he constantly feel fatigued?

Joe's wife, Sandra, had heard about Feng Shui from one of her beauty salon clients, and a little research put her in touch with practitioner Terri Stark. After having a lively conversation with Terri about clutter, furniture arranging, health, and money, Sandra made an appointment with her.

Terri arrived at Sandra and Joe's house [see Figure 8A] and

Figure 8A: *Joe and Sandra's home,*

was given a full tour of the home and grounds. Instantly, Terri could see a few Bagua areas that stuck out like sore thumbs [see Figure 8B]. The Health area of the house was a spare room, with a window that was covered with a thick blanket of ivy. In addition, piles of clutter resided in this room that, in some places, actually reached the ceiling. The Wealth area of the house was "missing," and a garage [see Figure 8C] that was crammed to the rafters with everything imaginable stood in the Wealth and Fame areas of the property.

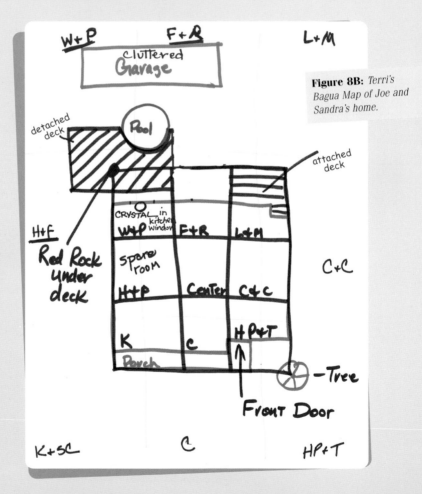

Figure 8B: *Terri's Bagua Map of Joe and Sandra's home.*

Figure 8C: *The garage sits in the Wealth and Fame areas of the property.*

"Get ready," Terri warned. "Here comes the clutter pep talk." She pointed out that the most disorderly areas corresponded perfectly with their complaints. "Your health and finances are both being negatively affected by clutter. The Health area of your house, and the Wealth and the Fame areas of your property, have become stagnant and essentially unhealthy due to the amount of junk there. It comes down to this: Clear those areas out and your lives will improve."

Joe and Sandra cringed when faced with the magnitude of the job. They'd been accumulating stuff in the spare room and garage for years. But the correlation between a chaotic environment and their health and prosperity was very motivating. So, they had their clean-it-up marching orders. Now what should they do about the missing Wealth area?

Terri located the Wealth corner under a freestanding deck that wrapped around an above-ground pool. After much discussion about what they could use in such a constricted spot, they settled on a big rock. Joe would roll it across the yard, paint it bright red to symbolize prosperity, and carefully place it under the deck.

"Now that's a personalized enhancement!" said Terri. "Try it and see what happens."

Figure 8D: *A unique enhancement—one big red rock—marks the Wealth corner of Sandra and Joe's home.*

Although it took both Sandra and Joe to roll the rock over to the deck, they did decide to try this unique enhancement. Once the Herculean task of moving the rock was completed, it received a thick coat of red paint and was ceremoniously placed on the spot that marked the missing Wealth corner [see Figure 8D]. As much effort as that took, it was nothing compared to the amount of energy the couple expended unloading years of junk from their garage. It's interesting to note that as they loaded the truck to go to the dump and filled bags with charitable donations, they felt better and better. Joe said it was like lifting a 100-pound pack off his shoulders that he didn't even know he was carrying.

Joe and Sandra cleared out the clutter in the house, too—especially in the spare room, where they also trimmed the ivy away from the window and added several lamps. Truckload after truckload of unwanted belongings were removed from the property. They hung a faceted crystal in the window [see Figure 8E] nearest the missing Wealth area with the intention of attracting an abundant flow of health, wealth, and happiness.

Shortly after they completed their handiwork, Joe was offered an administrative position at the school, which included a significant decrease in stress and an increase in salary. He and Sandra just looked at each other and hummed the theme from *The Twilight Zone*. This was the perfect job at the perfect time, and for the first time in their marriage, they wouldn't be barely scraping by every month. And, just as they were getting comfortable with this auspicious turn of events, Joe's grandmother decided to give them $10,000.

Figure 8E: *A round, faceted crystal hangs in the kitchen window to enhance the Wealth area of the house.*

Soon after Joe was settled in in his new job, he and Sandra decided to downsize and buy a smaller home. After getting rid of all their junk, they realized they didn't need as much space. They were ready to simplify. Their house sold quickly, and they bought a home they loved in the same neighborhood.

"We learned that having a lot of stuff means having to *take care of* a lot of stuff," Sandra says now. "We've simplified our lives and are free to enjoy every moment . . . which to us is the greatest blessing of all."

Postscript: Terri has since helped Joe arrange his office at work. Now, anytime he meets with someone on staff—from the principal on down to the janitor—they want to meet in Joe's office because "it's the best one in the building."

Summary

Joe and Sandra were suffocating under a sea of excess belongings. When things are chaotically thrown into a room rather than neatly organized and stored, they actually cause Ch'i stagnation. The more stagnant an environment becomes, the more difficult it is for vital energy to flow to those living there. This is a condition Feng Shui practitioners find all too often in our affluent Western society. In Feng Shui, every square inch counts. This is a departure from the popular belief that only rooms such as the living room or kitchen count, while storage areas carry little importance. As Sandra and Joe discovered, their cluttered garage and spare room correlated with their lack of health and wealth. As they cleared out these congested spaces—and their lives changed for the better—they realized that the "care and feeding" of countless possessions takes tremendous energy. They bought a smaller home and simplified their lifestyle, keeping only the things that met their needs. And they found out that a healthy house, like a healthy body, carries very little excess weight.

Feng Shui Tip

Bottom line: Clutter doesn't work anywhere, anytime. Let it go, let it go, *let it go.* You'll be glad you did, especially when the people and opportunities you wish for flow into your life. Ask these "Clear the Way Questions" when simplifying and organizing your possessions:

1. Do I love it?

2. Do I need it?

3. Does it reflect who I am at this time in my life?

4. How does it make me feel? What positive and/or negative thoughts, memories, or emotions do I associate with this item?

5. Does it need to be fixed or repaired? If so, am I willing to do it now?

6. If I'm letting it go, will I sell, give, or throw it away, and when?

Concentrate on surrounding yourself with the things that elicit a positive response every time you see them. Keep sorting and upgrading until your home acts as an "environmental affirmation," so that wherever you cast your eyes, you're greeted by something that has positive associations. When living with people who don't share your tastes, decorate one room or area in the home to completely reflect your tastes, encourage them to do the same, and compromise in shared areas.

(*Special note:* During times of transition, rent a storage space and keep it organized. Suggest to those family members and friends who'd like to store their stuff in your home that they do the same!)

Sandra and Joe's Feng Shui Enhancements

❖ Moving one big rock, painted red, to anchor the Wealth and Prosperity area of the house.

❖ Massive clearing of clutter in the garage and spare room.

❖ Brightening the spare room by adding lighting and removing foliage from around the window.

❖ Placing a faceted crystal in the Wealth window.

9

Room with a View

What do you give the man who has everything? Louisa was stumped, as that description aptly fit her husband, David. His birthday was coming up, and she wanted to give him something that would really surprise him. No ties, shirts, or cameras—this year she was looking for something really personal and unique.

When David mentioned that he'd heard about Feng Shui at work, Louisa thought, *That's it!* Thus, a Feng Shui consultation with Evelyn Seed became David's birthday present.

Evelyn arrived at Louisa and David's to find two very enthusiastic adults and one suit of armor awaiting her [see Figure 9A].

Figure 9A: *David and Louisa's unusual greeter, "Arnold."*

As Evelyn eyed the armor, David explained. "His name is Arnold. He's been in my family for as long as anyone can remember, and it was a great honor to inherit him." Evelyn studied Louisa to make sure that she agreed with what David was saying.

Louisa caught Evelyn's look and said, "I love him, too! I know he's unusual, but we think of him as our 'knight in shining armor,' and all of our friends know he's harmless."

Evelyn could see that Arnold was a definitive symbol of protection "who" enhanced the sense of safety and comfort in David and Louisa's city apartment. The welcome sign they'd added at his feet made him look less threatening. "As long as you love him, he's great," she finally conceded.

From the foyer, the apartment flowed from one lovely room into another. Evelyn noted that while each room was tastefully appointed with angels from Louisa's collection, there was no clutter to be found.

When they got to David's home office, Evelyn asked, "How's work?"

David paused for a moment, then said, "You know, it could be better. I'm in the mortgage business, and frankly, I should be making more money than I do."

From a Feng Shui perspective, Evelyn wasn't surprised to hear this. Although David's office was neat and orderly, there were two glaring challenges that were quite apparent to her. First, his back was to the door when he sat at his desk, which symbolized an absence of power and control. And second, a filing cabinet prevented the door from fully opening, signifying a restricted flow of auspicious opportunities in David's career. *This is perfect,* Evelyn thought. *The focus of his birthday Feng Shui consultation is indeed on David.*

Evelyn suggested that David unblock the door to symbolically increase the flow of good fortune in his profession. Because his desk was built-in, she advised him to position a mirror so that it captured a view of the door. "No matter how many Arnolds you have protecting you, you'll feel more in command when the mirror is there."

Louisa disappeared and returned with a red-framed mirror.

"How appropriate," Evelyn said. "Red correlates with the Fame and Reputation area, and that's where the mirror will be located in this room [see Figure 9B]."

Figure 9B: *A mirror provides David with a commanding view of his office door.*

Soon David was trying out his new view. "Louisa will never startle me again!"

"And your nervous system won't always be in the defensive mode while you're sitting there," said Evelyn. "You've just given yourself the gift of a command view."

Evelyn and David discussed his collection of memorabilia and enhanced the Wealth and Prosperity area of the room with some of his favorites. Evelyn also applied the Bagua Map to David's desk. With her guidance, he placed his calculator in the back left corner (Wealth), a paperweight award in the back center area (Fame), and a photo of Louisa and him in the back right corner (Love).

A month later, David received a promotion at work that included a salary increase plus commission. About a year later, Evelyn received this letter from Louisa:

> Dear Evelyn,
>
> Over the past year, my husband has almost doubled his salary, and I've started a part-time decorating business, which has blossomed and produced a second income for us.
>
> When I first heard about Feng Shui, I wasn't sure what to think. If you remember, I gave your consultation to my husband as a birthday gift. After so many years of marriage, I wasn't sure what to give him, but anything that would make his life happier couldn't hurt. He is much more at peace with himself and his life and is enjoying our increased prosperity.
>
> New doors began opening on a creative level for me. I'm helping people decorate their apartments, and I love it. As a result, David and I can now afford to travel and take weekend getaways together.
>
> All of the above is thanks to your Feng Shui consultation. It was worth every penny.
>
> Sincerely,
>
> Louisa

Summary

From a Feng Shui perspective, things that appear small can have a huge impact on the quality of life. Little annoyances—such as sitting in a chair that has no view of the door, or navigating through a door that is semi-blocked—take their toll. This is especially true when such annoyances are repeated day after day, for they tend to instill a sense of being power*less* rather than power*ful* in life. As David experienced, taking command of his space led to the empowering experience of a more lucrative position at work. Louisa also prospered when she put her natural talents to good use. And, as David and Louisa's work life improved, so have their opportunities to enjoy their leisure time.

Feng Shui Tips

1. Remove obstacles that keep any door from having a full range of motion. As easy as it sounds, clearing items from behind a door has proven to be one of the most simple ways to increase the flow of prosperity in life.

2. Arrange your primary pieces of furniture—such as your desk, chair, bed, and sofa—so that you have a view of the door. This does wonders for your outlook on life, as visual control of your surroundings empowers the psyche and relaxes the body. When this isn't possible, install a mirror to give you a commanding view.

David's Feng Shui Enhancements

- ❖ Installation of a mirror to reflect the home office door while David is seated at his desk.
- ❖ Removal of obstacles from behind the office door.
- ❖ Meaningful placement of objects on the desk and throughout the room.

10

Fine Dining

It was Chas who started it all. He was a high school student who had learned a few things about Feng Shui from a buddy of his. Chas then went on to inform his parents, Marc and Abby, that their Wealth area was in the fire pit. This was a pretty accurate assessment—Marc's career with a software company had gone up in smoke about two years previously when his employer's downsizing efforts put him out of a job. As the sole provider for a family of four, he'd been forced to take a job that he was overqualified for just to make ends meet. And when ends didn't meet, Abby got a part-time job. They scraped by while Marc looked out for another executive entry into the software industry.

Abby was very curious about her son's comment. She'd been wondering if there was anything to Feng Shui, and now she was motivated to find out. An ad in the Yellow Pages put her in touch with practitioner Don Fiore, and the following weekend, he was standing in Marc and Abby's foyer.

"Are you having any challenges in your careers?" Don asked, as he looked at the staircase in front of him.

"Abby must have told you," Marc sighed.

Abby gave Marc's arm a slap. "I did not! I purposely didn't tell him anything because I wanted him to see the house first."

"I took an educated guess after seeing the front of the house and the staircase," Don volunteered. "Your front entrance is recessed, and the stairs run directly toward the entrance. The recessed entrance is in the area related to careers [see Figure 10A], which indicates that few job-related opportunities can find their way to your door. Then the configuration of the stairs tends to create a cross-current, so that the opportunities that *do* make it here wash right back out the door."

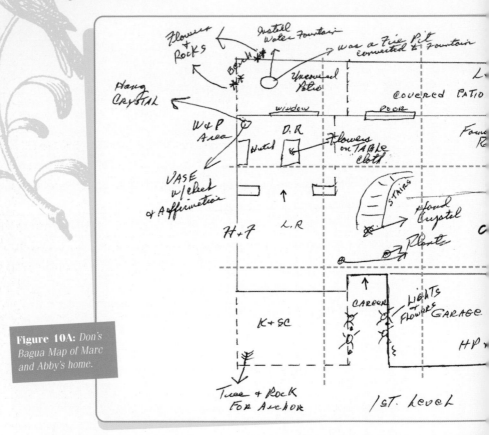

Figure 10A: *Don's Bagua Map of Marc and Abby's home.*

Marc frowned. "Is this Feng Shui-speak for 'you have a hopeless house'?"

"Absolutely not," Don assured him. "The observations I make are a lot like finding leaks in a roof. I find the leaks and recommend what to do to fix them. Then you have all the information you need to make the necessary repairs to protect your home—and your life—from any further damage. For instance, there are several things I'd like to suggest for this area of your home that will really help. Let's see the rest of the house, and then we'll talk about 'leak-proofing.'"

They toured the two-story house while Marc shared that shortly after moving in, he'd been laid off.

"I know they didn't want to let me go, but there were just too many hotshots on deck. When they downsized, I was one of those who got thrown overboard."

"I often wonder what the people's homes look like who keep their jobs, versus the ones who don't," Don mused. "I mean, the story you're telling me and the structure of your home are in perfect sync."

Abby picked up where her husband had left off. "Then Marc's father decided that Marc should sue the company for laying him off. But Marc felt that his former employers had done everything as fairly as they could, and he didn't want to get mixed up in a lawsuit. So Dad practically disinherited us for not suing. He's still barely speaking to us."

The three of them had arrived back at the entry of the home and stood at the bottom of the stairs. Don opened the front door and surveyed the space. "Let's get this area shored up so that blessings tumble through the door and *stay* here for a change. First, I'd suggest that you install lighting along the walkway that leads to the door, and fill the planting areas with shade-loving plants. The whole approach should be as beautifully entrancing as you can make it all year-round, so choose plants and garden accents that will really show off for you."

Don turned his attention inside. "In the foyer, you're fortunate to have space for a plant on each side of the staircase [see Figure 10B]. They will help to energize the space, and balance the cross-current of energy between the door and stairs. They'll also act as symbols of welcome. Put them in beautiful pots and keep them super-healthy."

"What do you do if you have a black thumb?" Abby poked at her own. "I'm excellent at drowning plants."

Figure 10B: *The staircase is enhanced with plants, a round faceted crystal, and artwork hung to create a strong horizontal line.*

Don smiled. "There are numerous things you can try. You could hire a plant service to care for them or buy high-quality silk plants. My personal favorite is to get a water meter and test whether the plants need water before watering them. You'll be amazed to see that most plants need far less than you think. If you don't like any of those suggestions, you could choose something else, such as matching statues, wood carvings, or a beautiful cloth draped across the banister. Just be sure not to crowd the foyer or you'll be creating another Feng Shui problem."

"I like the water meter idea." Abby looked at Marc. "Or maybe one of the kids will show an interest."

"Yeah, right!" Marc scoffed.

"The plants will love you, Abby," assured Don. "As for the stairs, they'll start to behave when you hang a round faceted crystal above the bottom step to help circulate the spill of energy. I'd also suggest that you rearrange the pictures that stair-step down the staircase wall. As they are, they accentuate the spill. Hang them in a horizontal row and they'll balance the descending flow of Ch'i [see Figure 10B]."

Don continued, "Now I'd like to introduce you to your Wealth area." They walked into the dining room and he pointed out the back window. "You see where the fire pit is? That's close to marking the corner. The dining room and the patio out there are your Wealth and Prosperity area."

"Chas was right! That scuzzy old pit certainly tells the tale, doesn't it?" Abby was pacing back and forth. "I knew we should've taken it out the moment we moved in, but somehow, it never got done. Well, it's history now."

Don held up his hand. "Now, hold on. I wouldn't say that you necessarily have to remove it. If the structure is solid, it could make a great base for a fountain, which is the classic enhancement of Wealth and Prosperity."

"It's solid all right. That's part of why we left it there," Marc said, as he stepped over to the door. "Let's go take a good look at what we've got to work with here."

A few minutes later, Marc and Abby had a plan. They would transform the fire pit into a water fountain and add a bench and a rock garden nearby.

"The fountain and your other enhancements will encourage you to spend more time out here and give you a much nicer view from the dining room," Don pointed out, "which should be the next stop on our Feng Shui tour."

Inside, Don asked Marc and Abby how often they used the dining room.

"It would be safe to say never," Abby replied. "We're the classic American family. We eat in front of the TV or at the kitchen counter."

Don wondered how many times he'd heard the same answer. "In Feng Shui, mealtimes are considered very special because we receive the nourishment that maintains our health and vitality. I'd like to suggest that you activate this room by using it at least once a week. More than that would be even better. Consider this room the one that gathers the energy of wealth, part of which is breaking bread with your family."

He looked around the room carefully. In a word, it was dull—white walls, gray chairs, gray carpet, and no art. On top of that, nothing in the room made a welcoming impression: The glass table was bare and had very sharp edges, and one wall supported a hutch jammed with a cluttered jumble of dishes.

"It's time to give this room a *rich* personality [see Figure 10C]. Okay, here's your list: Drape the table with a cloth in red, burgundy, or purple. Do you like those colors?"

Two heads nodded yes.

Don continued. "Put red or purple flowers on the table and organize the hutch by displaying only the pieces that make you feel very, very rich. Be ruthless in your selection. Choose one piece to display on a stand in the Wealth area of the room. Beneath the piece, place an affirmation that states your intention to be abundantly prosperous, and hang a crystal from the ceiling in the same corner to activate it. Find a painting for the room that complements the colors chosen for everything else. That should do it."

"That should do it, all right!" Abby was still scribbling notes. "This room won't know what hit it."

Figure 10C: *Abby gives the dining room a "rich" personality.*

Don added, "I'd suggest that you do the same kind of arrangement in the Wealth corner of your bedroom. Start with items that make you feel rich, and then put an affirmation beneath them and a crystal above them." Don smiled at his clients. "And except for one more comment about the front of your house, we're done!"

Out front, Don pointed out that the area related to knowledge and self-cultivation was missing from the structure of their house. "You can plant an ornamental tree to mark the corner, then landscape the area to feel more like an outdoor room, which will add even more magic to your front entrance."

Abby took Marc's hand. "We like that!"

Three weeks later, Don called to see how things were progressing.

Abby answered the phone. "I was just thinking about you—in fact, we've been singing your praises ever since Marc got the check from his dad."

Don had a strong feeling he was about to hear something wonderful. "What check?"

Abby's words tumbled out. "Well, let me back up. As soon as you left, Marc got right to work on the fountain. It was done in a week. Then he tackled the other outdoor jobs, leaving me to focus on the indoor enhancements. That dining-room hutch was something out of a bad dream, and I spent two days sorting through all the stuff in there, most of which was junk. However, I did find the Chinese vase my grandmother gave me—which I adore— and a few other treasures I'd forgotten about. Anyway, after a couple of weeks of accomplishing the things you suggested, the dining room looked gorgeous for the first time in its life. That's when I proposed that we have Marc's father over for dinner.

"You may remember that they've been estranged ever since Marc was laid off. So Dad reluctantly accepted my invitation and was quite taken with the improvements we'd made. He's a 'Mr. Fix-It,' so he was very impressed with all of the things Marc had done outside. All through dinner, he told stories about teaching Marc to do things when he was a kid. To make a long story short, they bonded. Even the kids got interested and didn't leave the table the second they were finished eating. Then—you're going to love this—two days after Dad was here for dinner, he sent Marc a check for $100,000, saying that it was part of his inheritance and he wanted him to have it now! He also sent each of the kids $7,000. I keep hearing your words: 'Blessings will tumble in the door.' Well, they certainly have . . . in a big way."

Postscript: The inheritance money was enough for Marc to purchase a business, and over the last year and a half, he has built it up to be worth more than a million dollars.

Summary

Marc and Abby's home had several Feng Shui challenges that pushed the blessings of life away. Don observed that the placement of the staircase, the lifeless dining room, and the unattractive fire pit in the Wealth area all contributed to holding financial loss and family estrangement in place. He was able to effectively address every one of these "leaks" and give Abby and Marc the direction they needed to do their own repairs and experience financial gain, family bonding, new opportunities, and ongoing success.

Feng Shui Tips

1. Ideally, every room in your home should be used on a regular basis. If you have a dining room, den, or other room that's used very infrequently, activate it by finding a reason to be there more often. For instance, "empty nesters" can turn an adult child's unused bedroom into a home art studio, hobby room, library, game room, or sanctuary. If you find that you "never" use a formal living or dining room, reorganize your activities to include it, as Marc and Abby did. It's also very interesting to note where the unused room is located on the Bagua Map of your home. You may find that the lifeless state of the room relates to an aspect of your life that needs improvement.

2. Staircases located directly in front of a door—especially a front door—tend to push away the vital energy entering the home. There are many ways in which this cross-current pattern can be corrected, and much depends on the space available between the stairs and the door. An abundance of space presents the opportunity to display an "island" of plants, furniture, and/or sculpture between the door and staircase. A smaller space necessitates choosing enhancements that don't crowd the area, such as textiles or other appropriately sized decor. Where space is very limited, a round, faceted crystal can be hung directly over the bottom step to help modulate the downward flow of energy. A mirror hung across from the stairs can also help. And, rather than stair-stepping art down a staircase wall, hang it to create strong horizontal lines [see Figure 10B].

Marc and Abby's Feng Shui Enhancements

- ◈ Enhancing the lighting, and planting a shade garden along the front walkway.

- ◈ Placing plants on either side of the staircase, and suspending a crystal over the bottom step.

- ◈ Hanging wall pictures along the staircase to create a strong horizontal line.

- ◈ Transforming the fire pit in the Wealth area of the house into a water fountain, with a bench and rock garden nearby.

- ◈ Making improvements in the dining room—including a tablecloth, a wealth arrangement, a colorful painting, and the organization of items in the hutch.

- ◈ Creating a wealth arrangement in the Wealth and Prosperity area of the master bedroom.

- ◈ Planting an ornamental tree and adding garden enhancements in the Knowledge and Self-Cultivation area.

11

Practice Makes Perfect

Judith Nourse discovered Feng Shui soon after moving to the mountains of North Carolina with her husband, Jim. Their decision to relocate was motivated by their mutual desire to enjoy a more peaceful lifestyle, but Jim also wanted to take a hiatus from his career as a clinical psychologist. Although he loved working with patients, the paperwork required by the insurance companies' managed care had become a nightmare—and so, tired of fighting for compensation, he decided to take a break. Because their financial needs were substantially reduced in a rural location, they decided to live for a while on savings and Judith's income. Although she was trained as a registered nurse, Judith would make her living as a reflexologist.

A glitch in their plan soon became obvious: Despite her considerable marketing efforts, Judith's home-based practice simply refused to grow.

"I sensed that there was something 'wrong' with the house and did some Feng Shui research to see if it had anything to do with my sluggish business," Judith says today. "I found that it did. The property sloped down from the road to our home, and continued its downward slant behind the house to a pond below."

As Judith knew, in Feng Shui, this location was far from exemplary. For ideal Ch'i flow, the best spot for a home is above a road, embraced around the sides and back by hills, trees, or other natural elements. A water source, such as a pond, is best situated in the front of the house.

"It was as if our house sat backwards on the property. To symbolically lift the house and improve the flow of energy, Jim and I installed a spotlight in the backyard that pointed toward the house and illuminated the roof. We turned the light on and said a prayer for my success. Within a week, I got more calls than I'd gotten in the previous month—it just lit up! All of a sudden, *everyone* wanted to come in for a treatment."

When Jim was ready to begin another practice, he leased an office in town and hung out his shingle. This time, he decided to operate a "cash only" practice in which clients paid him directly for his services. He knew that this was considered almost impossible in his

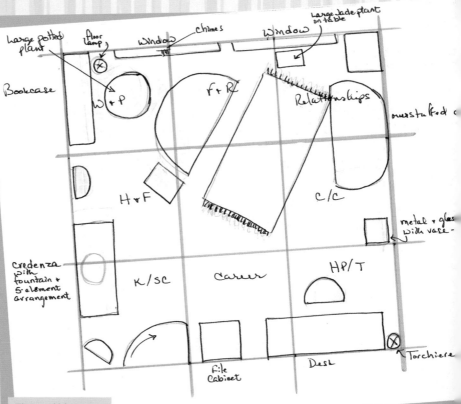

Figure 11A:
*Judith's Bagua Map
of Jim's office.*

94

Great Mystery, I ask that you send to this sacred space individuals who are sincerely motivated to receive healing and to engage actively in the process necessary to effect healing. I ask that you send individuals seeking to walk the path of individuation, to stay with it as we traverse difficult terrain. And I ask for your blessings on my life and my process of unfolding as I touch and am touched by the souls who enter here.

Figure 11B: *Jim's personal affirmation.*

profession, since most people relied on their insurance companies to pay the medical bills. For Jim, however, this wasn't an option. He planned to build a practice of about 20 clients in need of deep inner work—a practice that was small, simple, and rewarding for both patient *and* therapist.

Jim and Judith designed his office with good Ch'i flow in mind. They put a tabletop fountain on the bookshelves in the Wealth and Prosperity area [see Figure 11A], where Jim also placed the clear intention that he'd written [see Figure 11B].

Within a few weeks, Jim was working with several private clients and spending every Tuesday practicing psychology in a medical doctor's office. He was excellent at keeping his office scrupulously uncluttered and his files current. Even so, after six months and no increase in his client base, he decided that it was time for a Feng Shui checkup.

"We did a detailed inspection and decided to start by enhancing the Helpful People and Travel area of Jim's office," Judith recalls. "Here, we placed a new floor lamp and a list of people Jim was grateful for, which symbolized his intention to light up his practice and connect with the right people at the right time. Within the next few days, he noticed a distinct increase in referrals, which added more clients to his weekly schedule."

Next, Jim and Judith enhanced the Children and Creativity area, which is associated with encouragement and joy. "These were the attributes that Jim constantly fostered in his clients, and he wanted to highlight that area of the room. He chose a metal and glass table and adorned it with a colorful ceramic vase and branches [see Figure 11C]. He also hung a large wind chime in the office's window [see Figure 11D], symbolizing a plentiful and harmonious flow of wealth. In the next couple of days, he added several more clients to his schedule. While his practice steadily grew, I studied to be an Essential Feng Shui practitioner."

After her Feng Shui classes were over, Judith had an "Aha!" about Jim's office. "I realized that as a psychologist, Jim is really in the business of enhancing his clients' health, as well as their knowledge and self-cultivation. When I returned from my training, I noticed that the door into his office is in the Knowledge area, and because it opens to the right, clients aren't really greeted by anything. They have to get into the room and shut the door before the room welcomes them. That is unacceptable!"

Judith arranged a grouping composed of objects representing the Five Elements [see Appendix II] near the door into the room. On a teak credenza (Wood), she added the tabletop fountain (Water) that had been on the bookshelves, a candle (Fire), a polished rock (Metal), and a few ceramic figurines (Earth and Fire). Her arrangement welcomed clients as they entered the office [see Figure 11E].

Figure 11D: *Judith sits near the wind chime that enhances the Wealth area of Jim's office.*

Figure 11C: *Jim chose a table, vase, and eucalyptus branches to embellish the Children and Creativity area of his office, and a floor lamp to brighten the Helpful People area.*

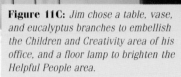

Figure 11E: *An arrangement of meaningful items that represent the Five Elements greets clients as they enter Jim's office.*

Jim's practice quickly grew to 20 clients, which was the optimal number for him. Now, he often receives calls from more clients than he can see in a week, which is appreciated by his colleagues who receive his overflow. Jim is also exploring his passion for Chinese medicine, while Judith divides her time between reflexology, Feng Shui consultations, and teaching Feng Shui classes in their community.

Whenever Jim notices that his practice isn't flowing well, he looks carefully around the office for the Feng Shui culprit. Recently, he found that an increase in cancellations ended as soon as he removed an unhealthy plant from his office. Jim acknowledges that most of his clients are people who take their personal growth work very seriously and are committed to improving their lives.

He says, "Generally, when clients are working hard to heal and are unable to move forward, I ask them about their home. If they're open to it, Judith will go over to see if there's something in their environment that's anchoring their problem in place. Judith and I [see Figure 11F] find that there are times when Feng Shui can identify the external dynamics of a client's home that may be hindering their inner healing process. In these cases, when the 'splinter' is removed and improvements are made on the outside, the person can heal on the inside."

Figure 11F: *Judith and Jim in his office.*

Summary

Step by step, Judith and Jim applied Feng Shui principles to create a successful, meaningful professional life. Additions that appear to be simple—such as a wind chime in the window or the elemental arrangement near the door—can make a powerful difference in improving Ch'i flow. Judith and Jim consciously interact with their environment, remaining sensitive to what it's "saying"—as Jim demonstrated when he traced cancellations to a sickly plant. Feng Shui knowledge heightens the senses so that we can hear, see, touch, taste, and smell when our environment is attuned and when it isn't. Judith and Jim know that the essence of Feng Shui isn't found in a single consultation or an isolated event, but in the intentional, ongoing observation and enhancement of our surroundings.

Feng Shui Tips

1. Homes located below street level can be symbolically lifted with lighting that's directed up to illuminate the roof. Weather vanes can also be used to "lift" the home, especially if birds or other winged creatures are included in the design. In addition, terracing the slopes is an excellent way to stabilize the land and enhance Ch'i flow.

2. Use the Bagua Map to guide you in placing meaningful things in meaningful places. As time passes, you may move things around to give them new significance, as Judith and Jim did when they moved the tabletop fountain from the bookshelves to the teak credenza. Use your environment as a game board of sorts, and enhance the areas that correspond with your goals and aspirations.

3. Watch for results, and keep working with your space until you achieve a result that pleases you.

Judith and Jim's Feng Shui Enhancements

- Symbolically lifting the house with outdoor light.
- Enhancing the Wealth and Prosperity area with an indoor fountain and affirmation.
- Placing a floor lamp and affirmations in the Helpful People area.
- Regular cleansing of space.
- Strengthening the Children and Creativity area with a metal table and vase with flowers.
- Putting a wind chime in the window.
- Creating an arrangement of the Five Elements to welcome clients into the office.

12

Room to Move

Monica had one simple wish—for her life to move forward! As it was now, she felt completely stuck. Her job in the financial department of a large company neither paid well nor made good use of her skills. Worse yet, she wasn't qualified for advancement in the company. Although Monica realized that her current position was giving her the experience she'd need to land a better job in the future, the future was taking too long to arrive!

To make matters worse, her measly paycheck meant that living alone was out of the question; instead, she had to rent a room in a house with two roommates who lived on pizza and videos. Having no taste for pepperoni or the latest in movie rentals, she was definitely the odd woman out. When she suggested that they share the cost of a Feng Shui consultation, both room-mates looked at her as if she was out of her mind. Why in the world would they want to pay some stranger to tell them how to rearrange their furniture? Monica didn't even try to give them an answer—she just called Feng Shui practitioner Becky Iott, explained her situation, and asked if Becky would come to the house—but only to look at her bedroom. Luckily for Monica, Becky's answer was yes.

A few days later, Becky was standing in Monica's bedroom. She immediately noticed that the door into the room was partially blocked by boxes, and that the room itself was crowded with furniture and even more boxes.

Monica caught her look and hurriedly explained: "Everything I own is in this room, but it's just temporary. I can hardly wait to move so that I'm not so crowded into one small space."

Becky could sympathize. "I know how challenging it must be to whittle your possessions down to the few that will comfortably fit into one room. But a cluttered area such as this one can hold 'temporary' in place for so long that it'll start to feel permanent. If you want to move your life forward, you're going to have to make room to do so right here in your bedroom. Right now, your extra stuff is keeping you stuck in this place. I highly recommend that you sort through it, and put what doesn't fit in here in storage." Becky paused. "But before you go out and spend money on a storage space, make sure that everything here is even worth keeping."

Becky went on to explain the importance of reviewing possessions from time to time, just to make sure they're still useful.

"As we change, our needs and tastes change. Things wear out or simply lose their charm. When they do, it's important to let them go."

As Becky talked, she noticed a computer and printer in the Wealth and Prosperity area of the room [see Figure 12A]. Knowing that work-related items aren't typically recommended in the bedroom, she asked Monica when she used the equipment.

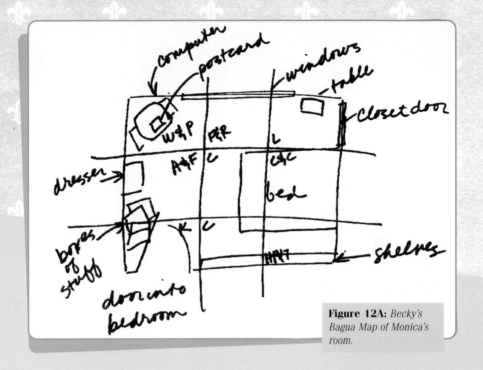

Figure 12A: *Becky's Bagua Map of Monica's room.*

"I don't use them at all because they're broken, as in beyond repair," Monica said. "I just haven't gotten rid of them yet."

Becky took a moment to consider the ramifications of this. Every time Monica looked at that computer and printer—which she did many times, every single day—she saw things that were *energetically* "irreparable." Buried as they were in the Wealth area of the room, they matched perfectly with the lifeless status of Monica's profession and finances.

Becky explained her observations, reiterating that excess possessions and broken equipment were the Feng Shui reason for Monica feeling so stuck. "Add a symbol of abundance to the Wealth corner right away," she advised. "It could be an expensive item, an image of flowing water, or anything that makes you feel rich."

Monica opened a drawer and produced a postcard showing ocean waves rolling toward a long stretch of beach [see Figure 12B].

Figure 12B: *Monica chooses a picture of the ocean as her symbol of wealth.*

Prosperity flows to me in constant waves.

Figure 12C: *Monica's personal affirmation.*

"That's perfect," Becky said. "Place it in front of the computer, and whenever you see it, say an affirmation to yourself that strengthens your thoughts and feelings about abundance."

Monica taped the postcard to the computer and thought about what her affirmation should be [see Figure 12C].

Becky checked in several weeks later to find out the good news: Monica had been unexpectedly promoted outside of her job classification into a management position, and was also given a significant increase in salary. She was now in a much larger office, and for the first time in her life, she had an assistant.

"Becky, you opened my eyes to the fact that my bedroom was really a storeroom packed full of old stuff," Monica acknowledged. "You motivated me to get rid of that broken-down old computer and printer along with a ton of other things. Then I framed my 'prosperity' ocean postcard and hung it in the Wealth area. Now I'm loving my new job, sleeping much better, not stressing out about money, and—you're not going to believe this—my room-mates want you to come and do the rest of the house!"

Postscript: Monica now has her own apartment and a new job that provides her with an even greater salary and better benefits than she received at her previous one.

Summary

Monica's promotion was a blessing waiting to happen. As she found out, possessions that hold little or no life force can prevent good energy from flowing in. Rarely do we find the "dead wood" of excess and clutter around people who are living happy, fulfilled lives. Monica discovered first-hand that clearing out the old enables new opportunities to take root and flourish.

Feng Shui Tips

1. Avoid keeping broken items that simply take up space. Whether "dead" or "wounded," they diminish, rather than enhance, the vital energy surrounding you. And, because every inch counts in Feng Shui, there's no good hiding place for them. Decide whether to repair or remove them—and *do it today.*

2. When circumstances are such that you can't move things immediately, place an item that's particularly inspiring in the cluttered space—Monica's ocean postcard is a fine example. This activates the Ch'i and initiates the process of positive change.

Monica's Feng Shui Enhancements

- ✧ Placing an inspiring image of the ocean in the Wealth corner.
- ✧ Removing excess possessions.
- ✧ Unblocking the door.

13

Wildflowers Within

At the age of 67, Jacqui wanted to be more financially secure for her retirement. A born nature lover, she owned and operated a hiking tour service, which specialized in wildflower walks catering to the "older crowd." This was her passion and she had no plans to stop, even though it had never been the biggest moneymaker in the world.

Although it had taken Jacqui years to save for a down payment, when she finally was ready to buy a home, the perfect place was waiting for her. She found a lot with an unobstructed view of a large meadow—it was as if nature's splendor was quite literally in her own backyard. Thrilled with her new home, Jacqui called Feng Shui consultant Katharine Deleot and said, "Come and show me where my money corner is!"

When Katharine arrived, Jacqui gave her the full tour, pointing out the meadow. "Don't you love this view? I can't believe I was so lucky!"

Katharine studied her and said, "It's really important that you *do* believe that you were lucky. You're already a wealthy woman—just look around. To successfully practice Feng Shui, it's vital to notice and be grateful for all that we've been blessed with. In fact, let's make a list."

The two women sat on the huge screened-in porch where Jacqui spent most of her time, and Jacqui listed the blessings in her life, including her health, her son, her grandchildren, her tour business . . . the list went on and on. "Keep it beside your bed, and read it at least once a day," Katharine told her. "Add to it whenever you think of something else. I mean, just the variety of wildflowers you can see from here is enough to fill up a page.

"Now, let's get to your original request, Jacqui. I'm going to show you where your 'money corner' is. Come on." [See Figure 13A.]

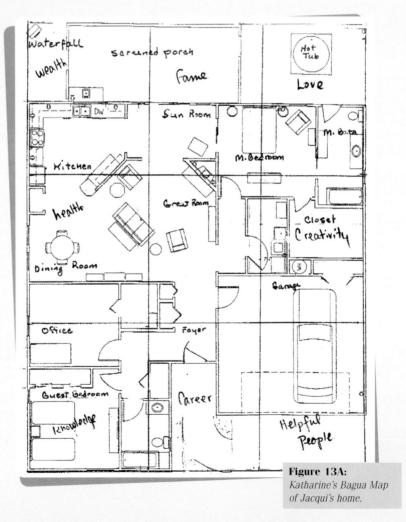

Figure 13A:
Katharine's Bagua Map of Jacqui's home.

Katharine left the porch and walked out into the backyard. She took a few steps and then stood in a patch of weeds and bowed to Jacqui.

"Great!" Jacqui said. "Could you just stand there and keep that spot energized for me? I'd appreciate it."

Not missing a beat, Katharine said, "Oh, sure— I have a nice red tent I'll set up so that I can be your living wealth enhancement."

She could see from Jacqui's face that she thought Katharine was serious, which made them both burst out laughing. "Well, maybe not me and my red tent . . . but how about a patch of red flowers or a waterfall that flows toward the house?" Katharine suggested. "Most of your Wealth and Prosperity area is on the porch and in the kitchen—it's just the corner of it that happens to land out here."

Jacqui promised to do something wonderful there, and they returned to the house.

Inside, they checked the Wealth area in each room, and together they were able to come up with some great enhancements. For instance, in the bathroom, Jacqui placed a shell filled with coins to symbolize abundance. She also put wildflowers in several vases on the living room mantel to energize the prosperity of her business. In her bedroom, she arranged her necklaces and bracelets so that they spilled out of her jewelry box [see Figure 13B] like a treasure chest.

Figure 13B: *Jacqui's jewelry box becomes a symbolic treasure chest of wealth.*

When they finally got to the front door, Katharine laughed. "This is usually where I *begin* a Feng Shui appointment, not finish it! But now that we're here, let's look at how you can enhance your Career area, which also happens to be your home's 'mouth of Ch'i.'"

She suggested that Jacqui bring her love of flowers into the small garden area near the door [see Figure 13C] and make the path wider with slate or other paving materials. Before ending their session, Katharine proposed that Jacqui come up with a wealth affirmation and repeat it whenever she saw one of her enhancements. "That way, you keep the inner and the outer Feng Shui in sync."

Figure 13C: *Jacqui's front entrance area, before and after.*

Jacqui's intention to enhance the Wealth and Prosperity area out back quickly turned into an industrious project. She bought a preformed plastic pond and installed it herself, adding a rock edge and a variety of red flowers. When nothing "prosperous" appeared in the first few weeks, she got help and installed a larger pond that featured a waterfall flowing toward the house [see Figure 13D]. Again, nothing "big" occurred for several weeks, so she called Katharine.

Figure 13D: *Jacqui's "wealth" waterfall flowing toward the house.*

I am now blessed with a constant and abundant flow of prosperity in my life!

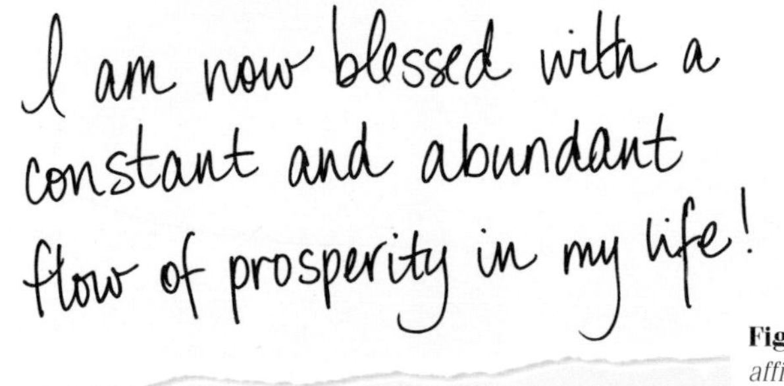

Figure 13E: *Jacqui's personal affirmation.*

"I have wealth symbols in so many places that I can't look anywhere without seeing one of them," Jaqui reported. "I thought by now I'd be a millionaire!"

Katharine thought for a minute and then asked, "What's the affirmation you're saying?"

The Universe will reward me with extra money," answered Jacqui.

"Well, no wonder," replied Katharine. "Your affirmation is all about rewards and extras in the *future*. Prosperity is a natural birthright and flows naturally to you *now* when you believe and affirm that you're worthy to receive it. Reword your affirmation and call me back."

Jacqui thought about it and came up with another, more appropriate affirmation [see Figure 13E], which Katharine approved of.

Two days later, an offer arrived that bowled Jacqui over. She owned a condominium that she'd been unsuccessful in selling, so she'd taken it off the market. Now, however, a gentleman was offering to buy it for more than she'd been asking—he also volunteered to take care of any necessary repairs *and* pay the closing costs as well.

Jacqui called Katharine at once and said, "It's working!"

The sale of the condo gave Jacqui a large chunk of money that her son, Neal, wisely invested for her. While her qualms about having enough money to retire began to disappear, her relationship with Neal deepened. They're now investment partners and find that they work very well together making decisions about how to "grow" their money. But better yet, for the first time since Neal was a little kid, he and his mom have become close friends.

"I sure have some biggies on my 'grateful list' these days," Jacqui told Katharine recently. "I see Neal and my grandchildren far more often than I used to. Even though the kids would rather play with the computer than take a hike with Grandma, we have a great time. And getting to know the man my son has become is incredibly rewarding. It's an experience money just can't buy."

Summary

Jacqui's story is a good example of how crucial it is in Feng Shui to align clear, intentional, *present-state* affirmations with action to get the desired result. Even with all of her enhancements in place, her affirmation perpetually kept her prosperity in the future—and, like a carrot on a stick, it was unobtainable today. When she shifted her thinking to accepting prosperity right away, Jacqui's life became much more satisfying.

When setting your intention for positive change, anchor it into the now by using present-state language. As an example, the affirmation "*I am now healthy, wealthy, and wise*" is fully accepting grace into my life now, while "*I will be healthy, wealthy, and wise*" keeps my intention locked in the future. When you speak as if your intention for change is already occurring, you create a clear inner pathway for manifestation to occur now. Be careful about how you use language to create your reality. Terms such as "I can't believe how good this is," or "I'm always the last one to get a parking place," literally push goodness and ease away. Sayings such as "It's to *live* for," or "How in the *heaven* are you?" promote goodness and often wake people up to the importance of language. Inner Feng Shui resides in the steadfast use of the affirmational written and spoken word.

Feng Shui Tip

Cultivate an attitude of gratitude by making a list of the people, places, and things you're grateful for. Such a list will show you how rich you are *now*. Add to it and read it at least once a day. (A good place to keep the list is beside your bed.)

Jacqui's Feng Shui Enhancements

- Making a gratitude list.
- Filling a shell with coins for a Wealth enhancement.
- Placing fresh flowers on her living room mantel.
- Creating a "treasure chest" out of a jewelry box.
- Putting an outdoor waterfall in the Wealth area of her property.
- Enhancing the front garden and walkway.
- Creating a personal, present-state affirmation for prosperity.

14

Living Color

Pam Stutzman was delighted to lend a helping hand to Reach, an organization that assisted so many in its community. The director of Reach had asked her to "Feng Shui" the location of their new thrift store. Since they provided victims of domestic abuse and assault with safe houses and other support programs, it was clear that Reach's heart was in the right place. But their thrift store had faced many challenges, including a high rate of employee burnout, petty theft, volunteer management problems, and (until now) a location that was too small for its needs.

Pam met with Jean, Reach's director, at the store's new site. Jean ushered Pam into a large, vacant space that had previously been a jazz nightclub—the interior of which was entirely black and white [see Figure 14A]. The former club contained two raised stages in the main area, and two large rooms, a bathroom, and a tiny office in the back.

Figure 14A: *A former jazz club becomes the site of Reach's new thrift store.*

Figure 14B: *Pam's Bagua Map of Reach's building.*

"This place scares me," Jean confided. "It's so much bigger than I'm used to—and so devoid of color. It's like being inside a giant black-and-white TV set!"

Pam stood in the middle of the main area and looked around with her Feng Shui eyes. "I see what you mean, but I also see this place as pure magic waiting to happen."

They continued their tour while Jean described a day in the life of the thrift store. Reach received an average of 70 bags of donations a day—most of which were wrinkled, stained, or broken. About 70 percent was salvageable, but the rest was too damaged and had to be thrown away.

Jean sighed. "I have to keep reminding the staff that going through other people's giveaways is serving a good cause. It does get depressing sometimes."

Pam could only imagine. "We're going to fix that," she assured her. "My objective here is to help you create an environment that supports and energizes *everyone*—you, your staff, your customers, and your donors." She pictured the new space full of light, color, and uplifting images. "Tell me what *you* envision for this store."

Jean listed her goals, which included an increase in sales and a decrease in shoplifting, harmonious staff and volunteer relations, and more effective community education and outreach.

Pam had some great ideas on how to proceed. First, she suggested that the receiving/sorting room be painted bright coral, which was Jean's favorite color. "Coral will help to keep the Ch'i flowing among so many used items, and it's a color that's associated with both of the Bagua areas that are located in this room—Fame and Reputation, and Love and Marriage [see Figure 14B]."

Jean was delighted.

Next, Pam identified the laundry room as the Wealth and Prosperity area, and suggested that it be painted purple, with a huge mural of mountains, trees, and a river on one wall. "I'm going to ask some of my artist buddies to help me paint the mural to activate the flow of prosperity. You watch—this is going to be a very enjoyable place."

They moved into the main room, where Pam identified the Children and Creativity area as being on one of the two stages. "In the Feng Shui tradition, this is the area associated with joy and encouragement, so it's an ideal spot for the children's clothing section. Let's do something playful here that will inspire parents and kids . . . like a *Wizard of Oz* theme. Dorothy is a good role model because she reminds us that dreams really can come true.

"Then, your dressing rooms will be right next to the children's corner in the Helpful People area. It has just the right energy for helping your customers find and buy what they need." Pam smiled. "And as a bonus, the location near the cash register will help deter any shoplifters."

Pam walked over to the other stage and identified it as the Bagua area related to health and family. "This is the area associated with a strong, positive self-image. Let's make this the upscale spot for your dressy clothes and accessories."

At the cash register area, Pam suggested that an inspiring quote be framed and displayed where customers could see it, so they would leave with a good impression and be encouraged to return.

Jean chuckled. "Boy, you're on a roll! I didn't know Feng Shui was going to be this . . . well, *fun.*"

Pam joined in the laughter, and the two women reviewed all of the proposed changes. Pam made a date to return, but this time as an artist.

Figure 14C: *A before-and-after look at Reach's new store.*

As soon as she got home, Pam called her artist friends and found three who were willing to donate a day or two of their creative time to the project. It ended up taking them a day and a half to complete the transformation. And, as the brilliant colors and shapes brought the building to life, Pam could see the dreams of many people coming alive.

Jean arrived with a reporter from the local newspaper, and they walked around the site with their mouths open. Bright hues wrapped the entire space in a kaleidoscope of purple, coral, cayenne red, turquoise, and gold [see Figure 14C]. Three whimsical canvasses smiled from the children's section: Dorothy in her ruby slippers; the trio of the Tin Man, the Lion, and the Scarecrow; and the Good Witch of the North [see Figure 14D].

Figure 14D: *Artists Linda Simcox (top left) and Judith Kaiser contribute their time and talent to painting the* Wizard of Oz *art for the children's area of the store.*

In addition, the dressing rooms were decked out in a medley of colors [see Figure 14E], and the upscale section looked more like a trendy apparel shop than a thrift store [see Figure 14F]. Canvasses depicting runway models—reminiscent of Erté's elegant fashion designs from the Art Deco era—flanked the door into the Wealth area; another painting in that part of the store featured a bride with her rainbow of attendants. Painted pegboards mounted in different areas would serve as colorful displays for clothing.

Figure 14E: *Color brings new life to the dressing-room area.*

Figure 14F: *Artist J. Jay Joannides paints a bride and her rainbow of attendants for the dressy-clothes area of the store.*

Jean wandered back to the Wealth and Prosperity area to find mountains and a tumbling river in the laundry room [see Figure 14G]. Wide-eyed, she turned to the artists and said, "This place is unrecognizable. People are going to absolutely love it!"

Figure 14G: *Pam lends her artistic talents to the "wealth mural" in the laundry room.*

The next day, the Reach Thrift Boutique and More was featured in the local newspaper, bringing the organization a tide of recognition, along with support from the community. A few days later, Pam met with the staff to help them bless the space. Together, they rang bells, burned special incense, and said prayers asking that prosperity and success bless all of their endeavors. A week later, Reach moved into its new home—complete with a logo and signage outside that matched the colorful palette inside.

After several months, Jean called Pam with an update . . . and what a stunning report it was. In their first three days of doing business, Reach had brought in $6,900 in sales. This was as much as they had made in a month before their move. And, every month's sales since had more than doubled from the year before: October went from $7,900 to $16,000; November, from $6,900 to $15,350; December, from $7,500 to a whopping $16,700.

Jean sounded almost giddy on the phone. "It's like night and day, Pam. I've already met every goal I set for this place. My employees are happy. I have more volunteers now than I need, and we have a lot more people shopping here, as you can tell from the figures. Donations are arriving in better shape, too. It's like people are proud to give us stuff now. One guy even told me the other day, 'This isn't a thrift shop—this is an experience!'

"And as a final touch, we put Starhawk's quote about community [see Figure 14H] on display at the cash register and by the door where we receive our donations."

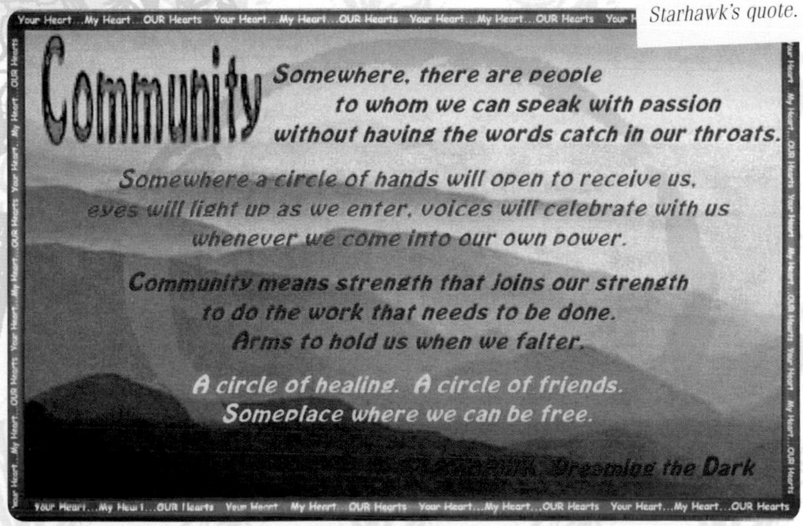

Figure 14H:
Starhawk's quote.

125

Postscript: Pam has since brought Feng Shui into several of Reach's safe houses, as well as to other thrift and consignment businesses. She also teaches Feng Shui workshops that focus on the special needs of those in caregiving professions. Reach Thrift Boutique and More enjoys the reputation of being the most successful thrift store in its area, and is considered a model of success for other retail-for-charity organizations.

Summary

This story captures the other side of the Feng Shui coin, for it's concerned with recycling the things that we give away. Here, we see the cycle of material belongings turn from useless to useful again. As one person's needs are met by letting go of their "trash," another person's are met by receiving a "treasure" that's genuinely valued. In the best of all worlds, everyone's needs are taken care of in an environment that honors and celebrates the abundant cycles of life.

Feng Shui Tip

Art and color can be chosen to accentuate the various Bagua areas. Pam demonstrated this by choosing the whimsical *Wizard of Oz* art for the area related to children and creativity, and by selecting the color purple and a river mural for the Wealth area.

Reach's Feng Shui Enhancements

- ⟐ Painting the Fame and Love areas a coral color.
- ⟐ Putting the color purple and a mural in the Wealth area.
- ⟐ Placing whimsical art in the Children and Creativity area.
- ⟐ Using art and color throughout to enhance the entire space.
- ⟐ Finding an inspirational quote to place in two key areas.

15

Down the Drain

Joan had been out of college for a year when she met Martha Seidel at a party. Their conversation covered the usual topics, including work and romance—and it quickly became apparent to Martha that Joan didn't have much of either. When Joan found out that Martha practiced Feng Shui, she quickly scribbled a rough drawing of her apartment on a cocktail napkin and thrust it into Martha's hands.

"Can you tell me why it is that every time I turn around, I'm broke again?" Joan implored. "I make a decent salary, but honestly, I never seem to have *any* money in the bank."

Martha studied the little sketch and said, "You mean your money is spent faster than it's made?"

Joan nodded excitedly. "Exactly! Why? What do you see?"

Martha shook her head and said, "I have an idea what's wrong, but I won't know for sure until I actually see your apartment. It would be unfair to give you Feng Shui advice sight unseen."

Joan made an appointment for a consultation with Martha the following week.

Rough as Joan's party doodle was, it had indicated to Martha that Joan's bathroom was located in the Wealth and Prosperity area of her home. Sure enough, when Martha arrived at Joan's apartment and took a quick tour around, the area related to wealth [see Figure 15A] brought her face-to-face with a stark white, unattractive bathroom—with the toilet lid up.

"You have the textbook bathroom," Martha said. "The kind that can drain the prosperity right out of your life."

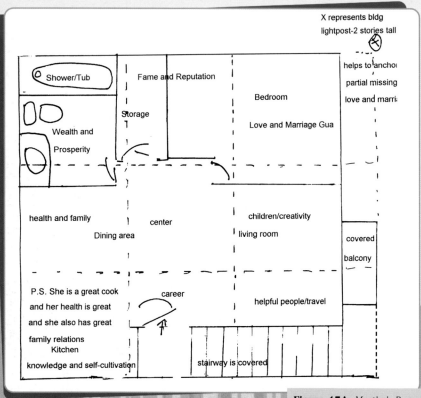

Figure 15A: *Martha's Bagua Map of Joan's apartment.*

Joan's eyes widened "I knew it! What should I do?"

Martha assessed the space and suggested adding colors that would give the bathroom a rich, opulent look. She could see the wheels turning in Joan's mind.

"Purple . . . I'll paint the bathroom purple!"

Martha agreed that purple was a great choice, especially since it's a color closely associated with wealth and prosperity. Joan was ready to run to the paint store before Martha had even finished her sentence.

"Hold on!" Martha declared. "You need to do a few more things in here, like keeping the toilet, sink, and tub drains closed between uses. As it is, the Ch'i is being pulled down the drains and—as you know only too well—it shows up in your pocketbook."

Joan immediately flipped the lid down on the toilet and pulled the stoppers closed in the sink and tub. Martha then pointed to the two faded, water-stained pictures that hung on the wall, and asked Joan to tell her about them. Each depicted a single flower, and clearly they'd seen better days.

Joan winced. "I picked those up at a garage sale when I rented this place. They were 50 cents each, which is about what I could afford at the time." Both women burst out laughing, and Joan continued. "I guess there's nothing quite like art that says 'Poor me' every time I look at it—and in my Wealth area, no less!"

A minute later, both pictures were by the door, waiting to go to the local thrift shop. Joan was itching to go shopping, but Martha still wasn't finished. Hadn't Joan said something about her love life . . . or lack thereof?

Martha looked around for the telltale signs of singleness being held in place. Sure enough, two pieces of art told the story: In Joan's bedroom, a dark charcoal drawing suggested a lone boat floating in dense fog; and in the living room, there was a painting of a woman standing alone on a windy hill, searching a vast expanse of emptiness. Martha smiled to herself and asked Joan what she saw when she looked at each of those pictures.

"You know, I've never really thought about what I see in them." Joan looked pensive. "The boat belonged to an old boyfriend who left it when he left me, and the woman is another garage-sale find. Neither one makes me particularly happy—they're just filling up space on the wall."

Martha pointed out that the boat in the bedroom was in the Love and Marriage area of her apartment, while the lone woman in the living room was holding court in her Career area. "Every inch counts in Feng Shui. Find a romantic or sensual piece of art to replace the boat, and imagery that inspires and empowers you to take the place of the woman. Then pair some of your pretty things together, like two candlesticks or two flowers in a vase, and put them around the house. Isn't it interesting that if you include the flowers in the bathroom, you had four 'lonesome' pieces of art in your apartment—and they were just about in every room!" Martha gave Joan an encouraging smile. "Looks like you'll be shopping for more than just paint."

Joan and Martha left together, and by nightfall, Joan had given the four "lonely" pictures to charity and was back home, painting the bathroom [see Figure 15B]. Her quest for new art produced a picture of a colorful garden in a gilded frame for the bathroom, a watercolor of a pair of doves for the bedroom, and a framed poem for the living room [see Figure 15C].

Figure 15B: *Joan turns the bathroom in her Wealth area into a purple paradise.*

I slept and dreamt that life was joy,
I awoke and saw that life was service,
I acted and behold, service was joy.

\- *Rabindranath Tagore*

Figure 15C: *The inspiring quote Joan chose to enhance her Career area.*

Within two weeks, Joan was rewarded with a bonus at work that was much larger than she'd expected. Soon after, a friend surprised her by repaying a loan that Joan had given up on long ago. She talked with Martha about her good fortune, and then wrote her a note:

Dear Martha,

I've been meaning to send you a summary of what has happened in my life since I spoke with you last, but new stuff keeps happening!

As I mentioned before, after painting the bathroom and closing the drains, my finances really improved. I received a much larger bonus check than I expected, a friend paid off a loan that I actually never expected to see again, and I got approved for a much lower interest rate than I anticipated on a personal loan. I'm also making incredible progress for the first time in paying down an old loan, my student loan interest rates dropped dramatically (with some thanks to the federal government), and there have been quite a few unexpected checks in my mailbox.

I'm also in a new relationship that's going very well.

Interesting changes have taken place, for which I thank you so much.

Joan

Summary

Bathrooms are classically considered "bad" in Feng Shui, for good reason. All too often, they're unpleasant, unadorned places with open plumbing that pulls your attention—and your Ch'i—down the drain. Treat *all* of your bathrooms, including the ones that no one sees but you, with the same design dignity and flair that you give your most public rooms. Give them a special personality that lifts your spirits every time you're there. In Joan's case, the bathroom is located in the area related to wealth, and its poor condition was influencing her money flow—when it improved, so did her prosperity. No matter where your bathrooms are located, their condition affects some part of your life, so close the drains and make them wonderful places to be!

Feng Shui Tip

For many people, part of the richness of life is in sharing it with an intimate partner. If you're single and wish to have a mate, replace art that depicts solitary figures with images that show two objects or people together. Pair items such as candlesticks and plants together and display them around the house.

Joan's Feng Shui Enhancements

◈ Painting the bathroom purple, closing the drains between uses, and placing lush garden art on the wall.

◈ Putting a piece of art depicting doves in the bedroom.

◈ Hanging a framed poem in the living room.

16

Full Circle

ooking back, Jeff and Sabrina could see exactly when their troubles began: Their lives had been great until they moved into their beautiful new house. Both Jeff and Sabrina had grown accustomed to a prosperous lifestyle—replete with good friends, plenty of extra income, and lots of lucrative business opportunities—and it was impossible for either of them to imagine life any other way.

The two were thrilled to have the money to buy such a gorgeous home, and they were looking forward to sharing it with their many friends. Soon after moving into their new place, however, they took out a second mortgage and invested it with a fraudulent business partner. When Jeff and Sabrina discovered that their money was gone, the emotional shock of being "ripped off" was surpassed only by the physical shock that awaited them when the dust had settled on their finances. Suddenly, due to the poor investment, a huge mortgage, and a brewing lawsuit with their former business partner, they were barely able to make ends meet.

The downward spiral began: With vastly diminished resources, stress prevailed; the added pressure decreased Jeff's productivity in sales and Sabrina's creative spark in advertising. Their income took a dive, so they could no longer afford to lavishly entertain or go jet-setting with their afflu-ent friends. Deeply embarrassed, Jeff and Sabrina lost touch with many of their old crowd, and this, in turn, caused them even *more* stress. While the couple's credit-card debt soared, their ability to pay bills plummeted. Just one year after the move, their dreamy life had become a nightmare.

One morning, Sabrina heard about Feng Shui on TV. She noticed that some woman kept raving about what a difference it had made in her love life—Sabrina decided right then and there that if Feng Shui could help save a marriage, it could probably help stop financial ruin, too. Within an hour, she had talked to and made an appointment with Christina Jantzen, a Feng Shui practitioner and interior designer.

Christina pulled up to Jeff and Sabrina's house, and before she even got out of her car, she could see trouble. The front entrance and right side of the house were recessed [see Figure 16A], leaving no structure to hold the Career or Helpful People areas in place. She recalled her phone conversation with Sabrina, and thought, *No wonder they're having such unfortunate experiences.*

Jeff and Sabrina greeted Christina at the door, and she was struck by how desperate they looked. As they showed her around, Christina realized that the house was broadcasting the story of their woes—for although the decor inside was beautiful, the shape of the house itself left four of the nine Bagua areas outside of the structure.

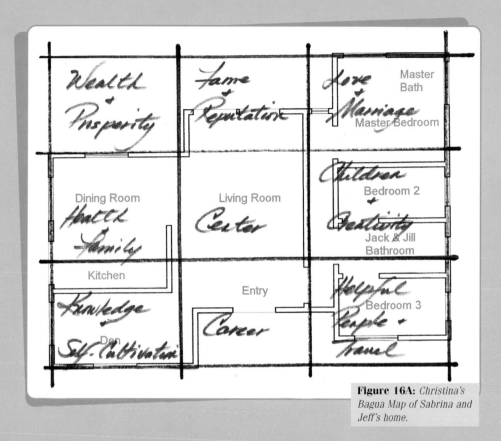

Figure 16A: *Christina's Bagua Map of Sabrina and Jeff's home.*

Christina had already noticed the missing Career and Helpful People areas in the front of the house, and she wasn't the slightest bit surprised that the other two missing areas were Wealth and Fame. She felt a wave of compassion for the struggling couple. "Your house is physically beautiful, but energetically challenged, as you've certainly experienced. But I'm happy to say that it's not a terminal case—there are things you can do outside to balance and enhance the energy flowing through the house. You'll know you're on the right track when your careers and finances start to improve."

Jeff rubbed his palms together. "So, Dr. Jantzen, tell us what to do."

137

Christina had Jeff and Sabrina make a list of solutions for their four problem areas:

1. *For the Career area:* To attract auspicious business opportunities to you, install a water fountain near the front door that flows 360 degrees, or toward the house.

2. *For the Helpful People area:* To attract "heavenly" people and circumstances, plant a "helpful" tree—one that bears fruit or flowers—in the front of the house and surround it with heavenly embellishments, such as flowers, a wind chime, or statuary.

3. *For the Wealth area:* To strengthen and hold finances in place, create a garden containing red, blue, and purple flowers and plants; anchor it with a flagpole and banner that symbolizes wealth.

4. *For the Fame area:* To assure professional recognition and acknowledgment, enhance the existing patio and furniture with pots of red flowers, outdoor lighting, and other favorite items.

Christina pointed out that this was a budget-conscious list. "You can get as fancy as you want with any of the areas. For instance, you could build a trellis across the back of the house to symbolically unite Fame with Wealth."

"Is that absolutely necessary?" Sabrina asked with a tinge of panic in her voice.

"No, it isn't," Christina assured. "It's something you can plan for in the future—when you're millionaires again."

Jeff looked miserable. "I'd settle for being debt free and being able to go out to dinner once a week."

"Oh, go ahead and set your sights higher than that," Christina encouraged. "Once the house is balanced, you'll feel as if you've awakened from a bad dream and have returned to the land of the living. Believe me, it's all going to be okay."

She was right. The moment Jeff and Sabrina focused their attention on enhancing the four missing areas, the nightmare began to fade. A week after they installed a two-tiered fountain near the front door, one of Sabrina's college friends came to visit . . . and before she left, she'd made all the necessary calls to land a huge advertising contract for Sabrina.

"We hadn't even gotten to the other improvements when this happened," Sabrina told Christina several months later. "My friend just walked in and changed my life. I'll be working with her company for at least the next year."

Christina was delighted. "That's how it happens—it often doesn't take much to begin to turn things around. Anyway, tell me the rest."

"Well," Sabrina continued, "Jeff and I created two new gardens. In the front, for Helpful People, we planted my favorite tree, a crepe myrtle, and added a large birdbath that has a statue of St. Francis of Assisi in the middle [see Figure 16B]. We never knew we had so many birds around here. We call them our 'helpful angels' because they like to stand on St. Francis's head."

Sabrina went on with her happy report. "In the back, Jeff got quite industrious. He took your term 'anchor' to heart and wanted to have a gazebo built in the Wealth area. We couldn't possibly afford that right now, so he made a rock garden. He figured rocks meant 'rock-solid wealth,' and put the biggest boulder he could find right where the Wealth and Prosperity corner would be if the house were squared off. He also installed solar lights and a flagpole painted gold for prosperity—let me assure you that this was no small job. Anyway, I found a flag in reds and purples and planted lots of flowers. When we were all done, we lit candles and said a blessing out there. It looks great, and Jeff's equipment sales are looking great, too. He's recouped several of his old customers and is really doing well."

Christina could feel Sabrina's excitement over the phone. It sounded as if hope was certainly growing in Jeff and Sabrina's garden.

Yet Sabrina wasn't finished. "We also spruced up our Fame patio with red table linens and flowers, and we're entertaining again, thank God. That's Jeff's favorite thing to do, and when we had to give it up, he felt like such a failure. We bought two special torches to 'light up' our reputations, and as soon as we put them in the Fame area, Jeff had the opportunity to entertain a group here from our town's sister city. It was written up in the local newspaper, which really meant a lot to him.

"Christina, what we've been through has changed us. I notice that Jeff is a nicer person, and I think I am, too. We've decided to drop legal proceedings against our former business partner, since it was just going to keep the nightmare alive. We'd have to spend every penny we earn on it, and it's not worth it to us. Somehow, we were able to let it all go and be grateful for what we have. Feng Shui is *amazing*—it's worked as much on the inside as it has on the outside. We're more appreciative of everything we have now, including each other."

Figure 16B: *The missing Career and Helpful People areas are enhanced with a water fountain, birdbath, ornamental tree, and statuary.*

Summary

From a Feng Shui perspective, the shape of Jeff and Sabrina's house didn't support them in maintaining a successful life. With no place for the Ch'i of Wealth, Love, Career, and Helpful People to gather, the house was unable to sustain those vital aspects of life. A house such as this can be likened to a body that has unhealthy or impaired vital organs: Eventually, the whole system will begin to break down. This is what Jeff and Sabrina experienced when the loss of their finances led them to also lose their friendships, creativity, and self-esteem. As they "healed" their home by defining and enhancing the missing areas, its vitality increased, and the Ch'i that sustains happiness and prosperity was able to flow back into their lives.

Feng Shui Tip

If you ascertain that your home or office has one or more missing Bagua areas, do whatever you can to anchor them in place as quickly as possible. Sabrina and Jeff were able to put a lot of their own time and energy into enhancing their home's four missing areas, with the idea of adding more structural enhancements in the future. The essential idea is to unite the "wind Ch'i" of your intentions with the "water Ch'i" of your environment so that "fair-weather conditions" or a new vitality can begin to manifest. Don't wait until you can afford to do the perfect thing—do something to activate the Ch'i flow *now*, knowing that it's moving you in the right direction. (See Appendix I on the Bagua Map for detailed guidance.)

Sabrina and Jeff's
Feng Shui Enhancements

⬧ Installing a water fountain in the Career area.

⬧ Placing an ornamental crepe myrtle tree, a birdbath, and a St. Francis statue in the Helpful People and Travel areas.

⬧ Anchoring the Wealth area with a rock garden, a flagpole, lighting, and some flowers.

⬧ Adding red accents and torches in the Fame area.

17

Wonder Woman

Karen was one of those executive assistants who was worth her weight in gold—she was brilliant, thorough, and managed to accomplish as much as two people could on any particular day. Yet it turned out that at her job, Karen was treated more like dirt than gold. She was paid a pittance and given very little credit for her "Wonder Woman" skills . . . that is, until she met Feng Shui practitioner Pauline Uhing at the gym.

Their conversation uncovered the fact that Karen was overworked and underpaid. "I do like my job—I mean, I've been there ten years," Karen said. "But I know I should be paid more for what I do. Can Feng Shui help me get a raise?"

Pauline said that it was certainly worth a try.

When Pauline stopped by Karen's office for a consultation, she discovered that it was a floor-to-ceiling study of clutter that looked more like a giant paper collage than a workplace. Every available surface—including most of the floor—was piled with files and books. Dead plants hung from the bookshelves, and a water leak showed visible signs of damage behind Karen's desk. Pauline collected herself, wondering how "Wonder Woman"

managed to get *anything* done in there at all. How much better would Karen do in an office that was organized?

Pauline assessed the Feng Shui challenges in the room [see Figure 17A]. A sharp corner jutted out from the Helpful People and Travel area, symbolizing a distinct lack of synchronicity in Karen's life. The water leak in the Love area meant that Karen's partner at work—her boss—was unreceptive to her needs. The Wealth area was decorated with dead plants and a bookcase that was jammed haphazardly with manuals and papers, while the Career area was occupied by another chaotic bookshelf.

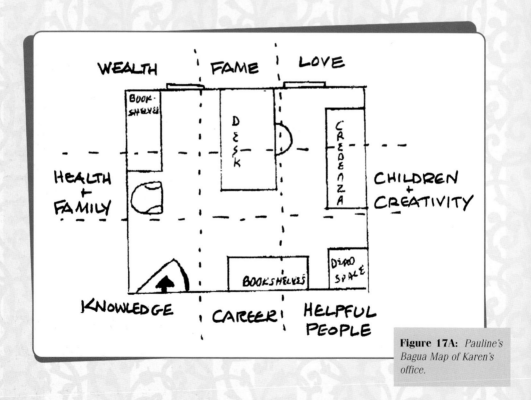

Figure 17A: *Pauline's Bagua Map of Karen's office.*

Pauline shook her head and said, "I've got to tell you, this room is doing a spectacular job of holding your problems in place. How have you been able to function in here?"

"With great stress," Karen confessed.

"So, are you really ready for a change?" asked Pauline.

Karen nodded an enthusiastic yes. An hour later, she and Pauline had dictated a prioritized list of things for Karen to do:

1. *Call maintenance and get the water leak damage repaired immediately.*

2. *Remove the dead plants and replace them with new ones—plants are symbols of wealth, so it's important to take good care of them!*

3. *Sort papers, manuals, and books on the shelves, desk, credenza, and floor.*

4. *Remove as much clutter as possible and completely organize the rest. Put often-used items on shelves and infrequently used items in cabinets.*

5. *Soften the corner that juts into the room with a wind chime, faceted crystal, attractive ribbon, or other enhancement of my choice.*

6. *Hang diplomas on the back wall, between the two windows in my Fame area.*

7. *Choose inspirational pictures that represent the various areas of the Bagua Map, and place them under the glass on the desk.*

8. *Display a personal symbol of power on the desk.*

Karen looked at the list with wide eyes. "When am I ever going to have time to do all of this?"

Pauline smiled. "At the speed you get things done, I'd say that one weekend will do it. Believe me, it will be well worth your time."

Taking Pauline's words to heart, Karen forced herself to go into the office the following weekend. Saturday night found her eating Chinese take-out between trips to the Dumpster. By Sunday afternoon, she'd pared her office down to the essentials. That night she brought in plants, a large bamboo wind chime, various greeting cards with inspiring images, and a small picture frame. She framed one of the cards for her desk and arranged the rest beneath the glass; she then hung the wind chime in front of the offensive corner and put the plants on the bookshelves [see Figure 17B]. Exhausted, Karen crawled home to bed.

Figure 17B: *Karen's "power office."*

The next morning, Karen arrived at work to find her door blocked by gawking co-workers—no one could believe how great her office looked. She subsequently found herself giving a short class in Feng Shui 101.

"I stripped my office down, and by Saturday night, it was completely bare," she told the assembled group. One of her co-workers raised an eyebrow and said that he wished he'd been there to see *that.* Karen ignored him and pointed to the framed card on her desk. "By Sunday night, I'd organized everything and added enhancements, like the cheetah power symbol I framed on my desk."

As people found their way back to their own offices, several of them asked if Karen would help them get organized. She told them that she'd be happy to give them Pauline's phone number.

Three weeks later, Karen started to notice all of her hard work paying off. She received a very positive personnel review and an excellent raise, and she was still basking in the glory of finally being recognized at work when she received a surprising phone call from a friend of hers. He informed her that he was selling his townhouse, and he wondered if she'd be interested in seeing it before he listed it with a Realtor. Karen had been to this house and loved it; another visit convinced her to buy it.

"I would never have qualified to buy the house if I hadn't received that raise," she told Pauline later. "And as soon as I had moved in, I was offered a new job! The timing's been so synchronistic—first the raise, then the house, and then a job that pays more money, requires less hours, and has fabulous benefits. Honestly, you were right: That weekend I shoveled out my office was the best thing I ever did for myself!"

Summary

It's interesting to note how clutter affects people's lives in different ways. In Karen's case, she was able to function in her chaotic office, but she was blocked from receiving the rewards of money and recognition for her hard work that she so richly deserved. The poor condition of her office was literally "the stopper" that held a heavenly life back from her. Because everything is connected, when Karen transformed her office to reflect her goal, she essentially removed that stopper, and many areas of her life improved.

Feng Shui Tip

Office clutter is typically made up of paper, paper, and more paper. Get into the habit of touching any piece of paper only once. This means that mail, faxes, notes, and other papers are filed *as soon as you receive them*—you'll probably find that the majority of such paper usually belongs in the "circular file" (the trash can). If you must save piles of papers, however, keep them current by culling them at least once a week. Bookshelves also need to be thinned out on a regular basis to remove unused or dated materials, for when you know that every single piece of paper you throw away makes room for prosperity to grow in your life, you'll lose all interest in surrounding yourself with heaps of it.

Karen's Feng Shui Enhancements

- Thorough simplification and organization of her office.
- Suspending a bamboo wind chime in the Helpful People and Travel area.
- Putting new plants in the Wealth and Career areas.
- Hanging her diplomas in the Fame area.
- Placing a personal power symbol on her desk and inspirational images beneath the glass.
- Repairing the unsightly water damage.

18

Life Is But a Stream

Carolyn Bratton unlocked the front door of the Lifestream Center and let herself in. The morning sun streamed in through the windows, illuminating a lush arrangement of plants across the room [see Figure 18A]. A memory stirred in her mind, and she stopped for a moment to follow it back in time. *Has it really been three years since I opened the door here for the first time?* she thought. She remembered how thoroughly pleased she was when she originally saw the space—it was so roomy and felt just right to her.

Figure 18A: *The Lifestream Center's inviting foyer.*

Lifestream, now a thriving nonprofit center for holistic health practices and studies, had certainly been quite different three years ago. Initially located in the cramped back rooms of a church, it had felt as if it was a growing kid who was

forced to wear last year's shoes. So, when the vitality of Lifestream dwindled, Carolyn decided to study Feng Shui and become a practitioner . . . and that's when everything started to turn around.

Carolyn knew what had happened. "My Feng Shui training opened my eyes to the fact that the Lifestream Center was stuck," she says today. "Its location inhibited our progress, and with nowhere to grow, there was nowhere to prosper."

Her realization had almost sent Carolyn into a panic. She wrote her intention down—to locate Lifestream in a vibrant center that would enhance the health, wealth, and happiness of everyone who entered there. Then, ignoring the tiny balance in her checkbook, she looked for a new site.

"The first place I saw was connected to, and behind, a beautiful Georgian home that housed a real estate office," Carolyn recalls. "A doctor had practiced there for more than 30 years and had just retired. The space included a large studio for classes, three smaller rooms for practitioners, a reception area, a bathroom, and a storeroom. The landlord even offered to 'put some money' into the place by replacing the ancient green shag carpeting and heavy drapes. I could feel destiny tugging at my sleeve—so I quickly ran some numbers in my head and then shook hands with the landlord. I just *knew* it was perfect."

Money flowed in from many new sources—from the owner, who spent almost $20,000 on upgrades; from the practitioners who rented rooms in the new center; and from students and clients who paid for their services.

"Much to my delight, I oversaw the improvements, making sure they were in accordance with proper Feng Shui," Carolyn recalls. "I chose a peach carpet to strengthen the Earth element and keep everyone in the center . . . well, *centered.* The smaller rooms were lightened and brightened with new paint and skylights. And as practitioners joined the Center, I helped them set up their rooms using the Bagua map as a guide. We hung diplomas and awards in the Fame area, put little fountains in the Career and Wealth areas, and used personal enhancements as 'beauty marks' around each room."

Lifestream was nicely settled in when the owner of the property called with a big surprise. The real estate company in the front house was closing—would Carolyn be interested in renting it? Feeling the pull of destiny again, Carolyn knew what her answer would be. Still, she wanted to do some Feng Shui calculations before giving her answer.

"I drew the two connected buildings [see Figure 18B] and placed the Bagua Map over just the front house. Sure enough, the Health and Wealth areas were partially located in the back house's studio, which meant that the real estate company had had no access to those areas. However, when

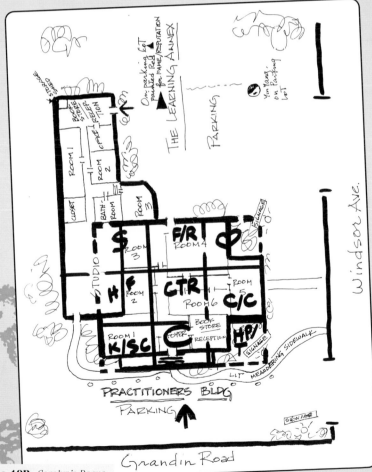

Figure 18B: *Carolyn's Bagua Map of the Georgian house.*

the Lifestream Center took over both buildings, the flow of energy would change. So, I mapped them out as one unit [see Figure 18C], using the main door of the Georgian house as the front entrance. The overall **L** shape of the two buildings together left three areas—Fame, Love, and Creativity—out in the parking lot. Portions of the Helpful People and Knowledge areas were also missing, and the Wealth area turned out to be in the furnace room. But it was all okay, because I knew just what to do."

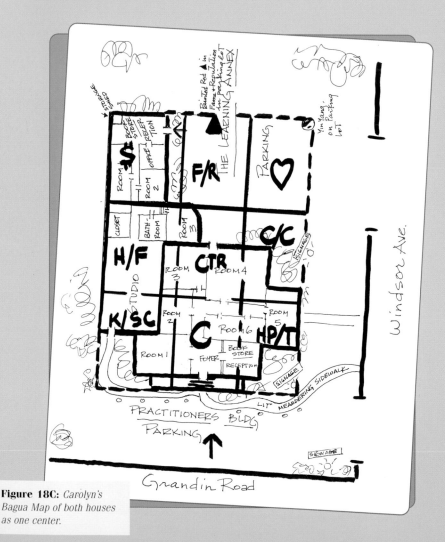

Figure 18C: *Carolyn's Bagua Map of both houses as one center.*

Figure 18D: *Carolyn stands near the front entrance of the Lifestream Center.*

Figure 18E: *Ahhhhhh, the massage room.*

Figure 18F: *Lifestream's reception and bookstore area.*

The first thing Carolyn did was have the front building's main door painted red [see Figure 18D]. In no time, various health practitioners, including an acupuncturist, massage therapist [see Figure 18E], and Reiki healer, filled the front rooms. She appointed the foyer with the welcoming sight of vibrant plants and a water feature; and included a bookstore [see Figure 18F], a tea station, and a large jade plant in the corner in the reception area.

Carolyn went on to clean the neglected furnace room and adorn it with lights and a basket of prosperity affirmations; she then placed bird feeders, birdbaths, and accents in the garden so that every window at Lifestream had a beautiful view [see Figure 18G].

Then came the signage. "Knowing the importance Feng Shui places on clear, attractive signage, I had three new Lifestream Center signs made," Carolyn explains. "Two were strategically located to enhance the missing Helpful People [see Figure 18H] and Creativity areas. The third was installed in a prominent spot near the street corner [see Figure 18I]. Spotlights illuminate them at night, which is especially important for people who visit us after dark."

Figure 18G: *Garden accents beautify the view from the massage-room window.*

Figure 18H: *A colorful sign defines and enhances the Bagua area related to helpful people and travel.*

Figure 18I: *Signage is prominently located at the corner to welcome people and guide them to the center.*

158

Figure 18J: *Carolyn employed symbols to enhance Bagua areas located in the parking lot. In the Fame and Reputation area, she painted a red triangle to direct Ch'i into the center. In the Love area, she used a Yin and Yang symbol.*

In the parking lot's Fame area, Carolyn painted a bright red arrow pointing toward the building to ignite the element of Fire associated with Fame and Reputation. In the area related to love, she painted the symbol of Yin and Yang to represent balance and harmony in partnership [see Figure 18J]. "It always amazes me how much better a place like a parking lot can feel with even subtle enhancements," she says now.

With the center in full swing, Carolyn turned her attention to advertising. She asked for advice from SCORE, a group of retired business professionals who volunteer their time to nonprofit groups. Their recommendation—to advertise on billboards—surprised her.

"I thought, *Who in the world has ever seen billboard ads for a holistic center?* But that was their point. Before any thought about cost could stop me, I called a local billboard advertising company. Talk about calling the right place at the right time! They just so happened to have some extra billboard space and offered it to Lifestream for free because we're nonprofit. Essentially, it was $17,000 worth of advertising, which made it the largest donation we'd ever received."

The paper costs for the billboards was $1,000—which one of Lifestream's supporters offered to pay. The billboards turned out to be very elegant. They had gold lettering on a purple background and said, "You Will Find Inner Peace at the Lifestream Center" [see Figure 18K], and "Zensational—Lifestream." In addition, Carolyn ran ads in the "Neighbors" section of the local newspaper to coincide with the billboards.

A flood of new business and donations poured into the center, and Carolyn, for the first time since the birth of Lifestream, knew that her efforts were paying off. Her "baby" was very centered indeed, and engaged in making a positive difference in the world.

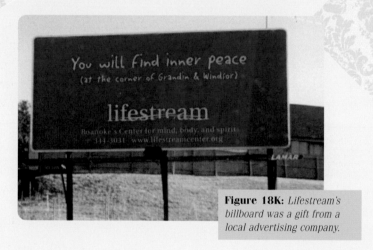

Figure 18K: *Lifestream's billboard was a gift from a local advertising company.*

Postscript: Carolyn offered the advertising company a Feng Shui consultation in return for their generous gift to Lifestream—and what she observed through Feng Shui eyes matched up with their business challenges. Carolyn recommended that they rearrange the office furniture to give each employee a view of the door. She also suggested less fluorescent lighting and more natural light; the removal and replacement of dying plants; and a thorough reorganization of the office's chaotic storage area. All of this led to a complete turnaround in the company's business.

As for Lifestream, it continues to flourish. Carolyn herself has also had another dream come true: After sharing a house for 15 years, she's moved into a spacious new apartment that meets all her needs.

Summary

Carolyn applied Feng Shui to her dwindling business and attracted great success. She addressed every room's furniture arrangement and elemental balance to assure excellent Ch'i flow. She enhanced all of the Bagua areas in some way so that there was no "weak link" on the property. Carolyn's dedication to high quality has created a healing environment that many people benefit from and enjoy.

Feng Shui Tip

Check the Bagua Map of a home or business you're interested in leasing or buying to ascertain what improvements will be necessary to balance the structure. Ask about the place's history to uncover unfortunate circumstances, such as bankruptcy or divorce. In almost every case, a building can be fixed if you have the Feng Shui eyes to see what needs to be done—and the resources to make it happen.

Carolyn's Feng Shui Enhancements

- ❖ New paint, skylights, and carpet throughout the entire building.
- ❖ Placing plants and other enhancements all throughout the center.
- ❖ Installing interior water features.
- ❖ Painting the front door red.
- ❖ Accenting the garden with birdbaths and bird feeders.
- ❖ Creating prosperity affirmations.
- ❖ Putting up attractive, well-lit signage.
- ❖ Painting a Yin and Yang symbol and a red arrow symbol on the parking lot.

Epilogue

"Dominoes"

Three days before this book was due at the publisher, my husband, Brian, was editing it for the fourth time. Suddenly, he slapped the manuscript down on the living room coffee table and disappeared into his office. I could hear him moving things around and decided to investigate.

"I can't stand having this old computer and fax machine in here one more second," Brian grunted at me from behind an armload of equipment. "I'm giving it all away." He heaved the pile out to the garage, and that's where his circuitous Feng Shui adventure began.

Apparently, when he got out to the garage, there was no place to put his rejects, so Brian spent the next hour clearing a section of shelves that, over time, had managed to accumulate a potpourri of extraneous things. Relieved to finally have the equipment stowed away for the next charity pickup, he returned to his office. The relief lasted for about one second—for now that the first layer of junk was gone, the second layer was in plain view. A variety of sports shoes, two lap trays, and various disorganized office supplies were now exposed.

Brian filled his arms with shoes and marched them out to the front hall closet . . . but there was no room there because that's where I had neatly stacked my desk's extra shelves. Brian, intent on moving the desk parts to the garage, spent a good chunk of time reorganizing the closet. He then took

a side trip through the coats, where he weeded out several jackets and a growing crop of excess coat hangers. Then he muscled the shelves out to the garage, where he cleared another space to store them.

Back inside, Brian opened the chest in the family room so he could put away the lap trays. But the chest was filled with the platters and vases that had found their way down from the kitchen cabinets. He tackled the cabinets to relocate the dishes so that he could stow the lap trays in the chest. When he couldn't find places for everything in the kitchen, he ventured into the laundry room, where he cleared a shelf to accommodate the overflow.

Returning to his office, he organized his supplies, found things he'd forgotten he had, and cleaned out his desk drawers.

Three hours later, after he'd reorganized seven different areas of the house and garage, Brian returned to his editing.

"I feel much better," he sighed. "Now I can finish your book in peace."

Appendix I

The Bagua Map—Honing in on the Treasures of Life

As the stories in this book demonstrate, one of the tools in Feng Shui that produces the best results is the Bagua Map [see Figures IA and IB]. By correlating the structure and design of your home with the blessings of vitality, happiness, and good fortune, the Bagua Map shows you how to summon positive change into your life. Many people have found that by following the directives of the Bagua Map, obstacles fall away, powerful changes occur, and blessings manifest.

The word *Bagua* literally means "eight trigrams." These trigrams form the basic building blocks of the Chinese Book of Changes—often referred to as the *I Ching*—and each are associated with important aspects of life, including health, wealth, love, and happiness. The Bagua Map charts where the Ch'i of each of these blessings gathers in your home. You may find that the good fortune you cherish, or aspire to, is being energized or depleted in your living room, garage, or backyard. What were two completely separate aspects of life—that is, your home and your "luck"—merge into one powerful highway that can lead to positive change and improved circumstances.

People have solved many problems using the Bagua Map. It's uncanny how often they find a correlation between their ongoing challenges and the way their homes are designed. Once identified, these people are able to take the necessary steps to transform the problematic "guas," or areas, and

Figure 1A: *Illustration of the Bagua Map.*

enjoy the results. For instance, in the story "Out with the Old, In with the New" (page 67), Sandra and Joe found that their health and financial challenges correlated with a cluttered spare room and garage that were located in their Health and Wealth areas. After they made the suggested changes and enhancements, their health and prosperity greatly improved. Similarly, in the story "Wonder Woman" (page 145), Karen wanted to improve her career opportunities, and after she enhanced the Wealth, Love, Career, and Helpful People areas of her office, that's exactly what happened.

Ultimately, the Bagua Map leads you to the discovery that *all* parts of your home and your life are of equal importance. When every area within and without is well maintained, uncluttered, and arranged to flow with ease, beauty, and grace, you're "home free." This applies as much to your inner world as it does to your outer environment. While you're improving and enhancing the outer "water Ch'i" of your home, look to see how you can improve the inner "wind Ch'i" of your attitude or character. Make the necessary inner "home improvements," as Jacqui did in "Wildflowers Within" (page 107), when she kept a gratitude journal to remind her of how rich she already was. This produces the most deeply satisfying and long-lasting results, and attracts blessings and fair-weather conditions into every facet of your life.

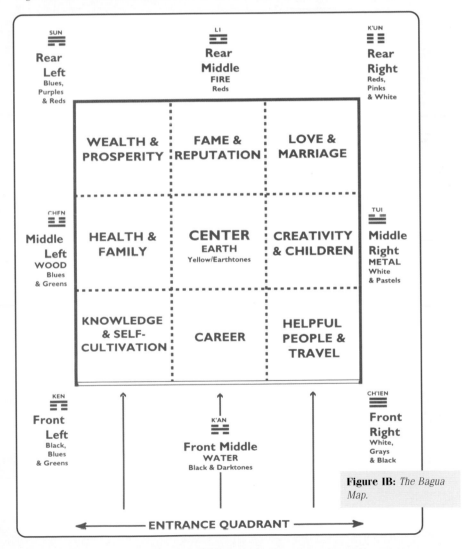

Figure IB: *The Bagua Map.*

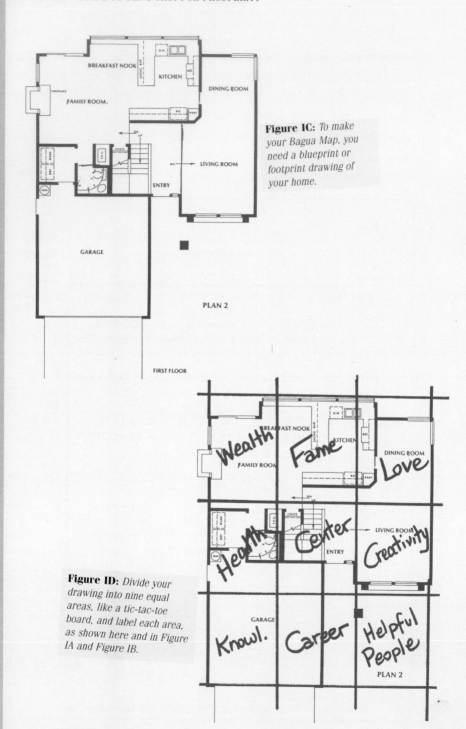

Figure 1C: *To make your Bagua Map, you need a blueprint or footprint drawing of your home.*

Figure 1D: *Divide your drawing into nine equal areas, like a tic-tac-toe board, and label each area, as shown here and in Figure 1A and Figure 1B.*

168

Mapping the Bagua

The Bagua Map can be applied to any fixed shape, including buildings, rooms, and pieces of property. These instructions are geared toward mapping your home, and once you understand the basics, you can apply the map to any structure or parcel of land. To start, you'll need a bird's-eye drawing of your home, such as the blueprint or footprint sketch shown in Figure IC. Determine the overall shape of your home by including all structures that are attached to it, such as garages, porches, room additions, arbors, storage units, and decks with railings.

Lay the drawing down, as depicted in Figure IC, so that the front entrance of your home is at the bottom of the page. Now, draw a square or rectangle around your home that's just big enough to include every part of it, as shown in Figure ID. This is the outline of your Bagua Map. Next, divide the outline into nine even sections, like a tic-tac-toe board, and label the nine squares [see Figures IB and ID]. This is your complete Bagua Map.

If your home has more than one story—partial or full—translate the Bagua Map of the main floor directly up or down to other levels, as shown in Figure IE. Multiple floors give you multiple opportunities to enhance certain Bagua areas in your home, but you only have to be concerned with having all of the Bagua areas represented on the main floor.

When your house is a simple rectangle [see Figure IF], you'll find that all of the Bagua areas are located inside the structure of your home. If your home is any other shape, such as an L, S, T, or U, you'll find areas located within the rectangular outline of the Bagua Map, but outside the structure of your house.

Whether indoors or outdoors, it's very important to determine each area's location. For instance, the home pictured in Figure ID is missing the Helpful People and Travel areas, as well as some of the Career, Wealth, and Love areas.

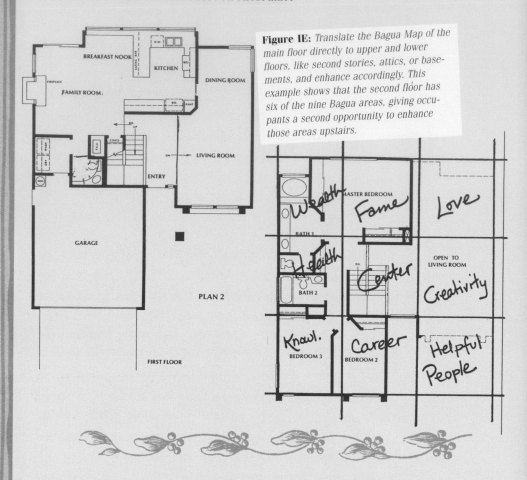

Figure IE: *Translate the Bagua Map of the main floor directly to upper and lower floors, like second stories, attics, or basements, and enhance accordingly. This example shows that the second floor has six of the nine Bagua areas, giving occupants a second opportunity to enhance those areas upstairs.*

Figure IF: *This basic sketch of a rectangular home, with its front entrance located in the Knowledge and Self-Cultivation area of the Bagua Map, has all of the Bagua areas contained within the physical structure of the house.*

W&P	F&R	L&M
H&F	CENTER	C&C
K&SC	C	HP&T

Front Entrance

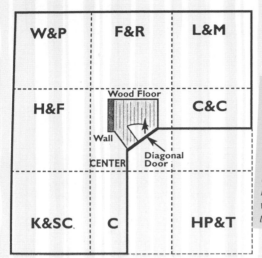

Figure IG: *This is a sketch of a home with a diagonal door. The foyer wall, floor covering, and direction in which the door opens help determine which way to map the house.*

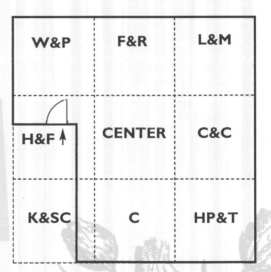

Figure IH: *This recessed front door is located in the Health and Family area of this Home's Bagua Map. Notice that a portion of Health and Family, and Knowledge and Self-Cultivation, are outside of the home's structure.*

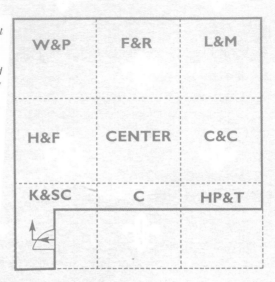

Figure II: *When a front door is recessed to the very back of the house, the Bagua Map is turned to fit over the main body of the house, as seen here. Notice that part of Knowledge and Self-Cultivation, Career, and Helpful People and Travel are missing from the structure of the house.*

Clarifying Points

1. Don't be concerned about where the walls are located inside the house. As you can see in Figure ID, sometimes one large room will subdivide into two or three Bagua areas, or one Bagua area might encompass two or three small rooms.

2. When your front door is built on a diagonal, use walls, flooring, or the direction you see first when you open the front door to determine which way to map the house, as shown in Figure IG.

3. When your front door is recessed past the front wall of the house, you may be entering your home through the Health and Family, Center, or Children and Creativity areas of the Bagua Map, as in Figure IH. If your front door is recessed to the very back, turn the Bagua Map to fit over the main body of the house, as shown in Figure II.

4. Because the home is larger than each room, it holds more Ch'i. Therefore, work first with the Bagua Map of the home, and then with each room.

5. Consult a Feng Shui practitioner if you need help making a Bagua Map of your home. (See the back of the book in order to locate a practitioner near you.)

Missing Areas of the Bagua Map

When there are Bagua areas outside the physical structure of your home, it's important to define and enhance them in some way. This can be as simple as installing an outdoor lamppost, ornamental tree, water feature, or large statue where the corner would be if the structure were rectangular. For example, in the story "Wind, Water, and Wealth" (page 41), Judy installed a waterfall to anchor the Wealth and Prosperity area that was missing from the structure of her home. Enhancements   such as flagpoles, large boulders, trees, fences, water features, and outdoor sculptures—can be grouped to enhance the area and increase the Ch'i flow in and around your home. We see this kind of creative arrangement in the story "Full Circle" (page 135), when Jeff and Sabrina installed a flagpole, lighting, and rock garden in their outdoor Wealth area.

A Bagua area can also be defined by adding a deck, patio, arbor, or room—such as the "garden room" Carol designed to fill in the missing Wealth area of her home in "Door Number One" (page 29). The goal is to anchor or complete the missing area with something significant that's in harmony with your personal tastes, pocketbook, and home.

Personalizing Your Choices

Whenever you can, choose items and designs that relate to the Bagua area you're working with and that have personal appeal. As an example, the photograph on page 112, from "Wildflowers Within," shows the water feature Jacqui built to represent an abundance of wealth and prosperity flowing into her home. In "Living Color" (see page 117), Pam worked closely with the Bagua colors and themes, including the use of whimsical art in the Children and Creativity area. In "Life Is But a Stream" (page 153), Carolyn incorporated attractive signage to define her building's missing Helpful People and Travel area. There's no end to the creative possibilities you can choose as you anchor the Bagua areas found outside the structure of your home.

When You Can't Do Anything Outside

Don't be discouraged if you can't do anything substantial to enhance the Bagua on the outside of your home. There are still many ways you can symbolically complete a missing area.

Symbolic Enhancements

Missing Bagua areas can be completed energetically by "planting" a natural quartz crystal where the corner or wall of the house would be if it were a rectangle [see Figure IJ]. A good example of this kind of symbolic enhancement is in "Patented Glory" (page 57), when Dory buried crystals to enhance the Wealth and the Fame areas of her business. Bury the crystal, point up, an inch below the ground, with the intention of lifting and strengthening the Ch'i. Your intention, coupled with the crystal, strengthens and supports the area that's missing in the structure.

Another idea is to use paint instead of a crystal to mark the spot, especially if pavement covers the missing area. For instance, in "Life Is But a Stream" (page 153), Carolyn found that her building's Fame and Love areas were situated in the parking lot, so she painted a red arrow in the Fame area and a Yin and Yang symbol in the Love area to symbolically hold them in place. Be as subtle or as creative as you'd like—and keep in mind that your intention to positively influence the flow of Ch'i, combined with the physical act of marking the spot, makes your enhancement powerful.

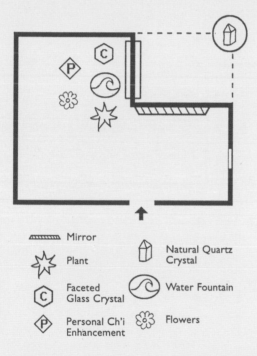

Figure IJ: *When you can't do anything "big" outside, find the missing corner and energize it by burying a natural quartz crystal pointed up an inch below the ground. Or, paint pavement with a meaningful symbol, circle, or line to mark the spot. Work from the inside by hanging a mirror or art with depth on the wall closest to the missing area to symbolically open up the space. Or use plants, flowers, water fountains, crystals, or personal Ch'i enhancements to build and increase the energy in the area.*

Mirror

Plant

Faceted Glass Crystal

Personal Ch'i Enhancement

Natural Quartz Crystal

Water Fountain

Flowers

Indoors, hang a mirror or art with depth on the wall closest to the missing area. This symbolically opens up the space to include what's missing. Or, use color and other decorative items to power up the windows and walls located near missing guas. It's also very important to pay special attention to improving and enhancing the Bagua areas in each room that correlate

175

with those missing in your home's structure. Many times, the same area that's missing in the structure of the house is also challenging in each room. For instance, a home that's missing the Wealth and Prosperity area often has cluttered closets, unhealthy plants, and disliked possessions located in the wealth areas of various rooms in the house. We saw this in the story "Out with the Old, In with the New" (page 67). The Wealth area of Sandra and Joe's home was missing, and chaos also reigned in several other areas related to money in their home. Make absolutely sure that nothing in your home is holding an unfortunate situation in place.

Mapping the Bagua in Every Room

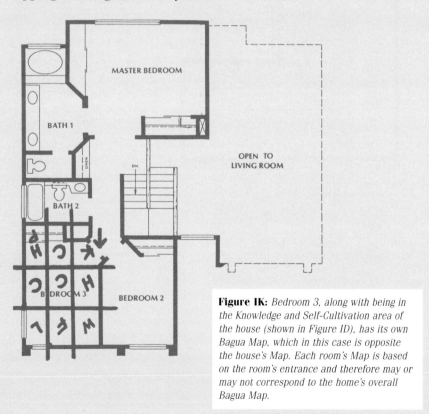

Figure 1K: *Bedroom 3, along with being in the Knowledge and Self-Cultivation area of the house (shown in Figure 1D), has its own Bagua Map, which in this case is opposite the house's Map. Each room's Map is based on the room's entrance and therefore may or may not correspond to the home's overall Bagua Map.*

When mapping a single room, follow the same steps that you used when mapping your home. Draw the footprint of the room and place the main door in the room at the bottom of the page. Next, mark a rectangle around the perimeter, divide it into nine equal parts, and label each section according to the Bagua Map. If there's more than one entrance into a room, choose the one that's used most often—if they seem to be used equally, simply choose one of the doors as the entrance for mapping the Bagua of the room.

Please note that the Bagua Maps of your home and of each room often won't coincide. The door or entry into a space is your guide when making a Bagua Map, and each room can be individually mapped and enhanced accordingly. For example, Figure IK shows a bedroom located in the Knowledge and Self-Cultivation area of the house's Bagua Map. But, as you can see, it also has its own room-sized map. You can take both the house and room maps into consideration when decorating the space: For instance, this room would make an excellent home office, study, library, or meditation room, given its location in the house's map. As a bedroom, it supports the study practices of a school-aged child. No matter how the room is used, you can place art, furnishings, and other decorative items to enhance the room's Bagua Map. An example of this is in the story "Law and a New Order" (page 9), when Maria placed her jewelry cabinet and other meaningful enhancements in the Wealth area of her bedroom.

Assessing Your Bagua Map Profile

Take a good look at each Bagua area of your home, then of each room, and answer the following questions:

1. What room or area is located in each Bagua area?

2. What possessions are located there?

3. Are they organized?

4. Do I love everything that I see?

5. Do I see a correlation between what's located in each area and the quality of my life?

6. What can I improve or enhance?

7. What's the first area I'm going to work with?

This can be a very revealing process! We often find that the condition of the Bagua areas in our homes has a direct correlation with that particular facet of our lives. Consider Gary, from the story "Soap and Mirrors" (page 19), whose financial woes correlated perfectly with the poor condition of the bathroom in his Wealth area. Or Nick in "Gone Fishin'" (page 1), who found that his "deadly" work pace was being anchored by the skull of a cow hanging in the Career area of his office.

This happens all the time—the objects we surround ourselves with on a daily basis are either nurturing us or they're not. If they're not, they may be holding unfortunate situations in place. Once they're removed, the Ch'i improves. Continuing with the examples from above, Gary wanted to enhance his prosperity. Bringing order and beauty into his bathroom and mirroring the adjoining wall to enhance his Wealth area did just that. Nick removed the skull and added a picture of the river that he really wanted to fish in—and soon that's exactly where he was.

There are also times when it's not that simple. When you want to change something in your life that's mediocre, unhappy, or stressful, you may experience chaos or lack of immediate results as a new order is being called forth. For instance, in "Wildflowers Within" (page 107), Jacqui discovered that her financial goals weren't manifesting simply because she constantly projected them into the future. She needed to adjust her thinking to affirm that her goals are met *now* in order to receive the results that she wished for. Working with the Bagua enhances the flow of Ch'i, and the enhanced flow will push whatever isn't working out into the open. If you aspire to excellence, everything mediocre or unclear has to surface first.

Bringing this ancient wisdom into your household can sometimes feel like a whirlwind at first, as the "Wind" of your intentions finds its way into the "Water" of physical form. Map the sea of Ch'i that flows through your home, and shape it to reflect who you are now, as well as all that you're aspiring to be. And get ready—it's my experience that the call for positive change is always answered.

The Inner and Outer Work Related to the Bagua Map

As you work with the Bagua Map, take the time to complement your outer efforts with personal inner development. Contemplate how you can improve your character (the unseen "wind Ch'i") as you surround yourself with improvements and enhancements (the seen "water Ch'i") that you love; don't settle for less! The more you personalize your choices, the better. Remember, your incorporation of inner and outer work produces deeply satisfying and long-lasting results.

Inner Work Related to Health and Family

Key Word: *Strength*

The blessings of Health and Family are associated with the I Ching trigram *Chen,* translated as "Shocking Thunder." Unexpected shocks or sudden unforeseen problems can cycle through our lives like stormy weather. We survive life's inclement times best when we're physically and emotionally strong. Physical vitality is assured through correct nutrition and exercise, while emotional strength is cultivated through the practice of honesty and forgiveness.

Honesty creates and maintains healthy boundaries—these boundaries include knowing when a person, place, or situation is "good" for you or not.

Life offers a wide variety of choices, some within and others outside of what's best for you. The quality of your life depends on your strength to draw healthy boundaries and know when to say yes and when to say no. *Yes, I'll meet you for lunch,* and *No, I won't spend the weekend with you. Yes, I'll drive to the seminar,* and *No, I don't choose to fly. Yes, I'd like to go to the movies, but not until after my exercise class.* While clear boundaries define and strengthen you, forgiveness is the force that keeps you in the present moment. You're free to move forward with direction and without heavy baggage.

Assess your exercise, sleeping, and eating habits, and determine how well you're maintaining the physical vitality of your body. Strengthen your emotional health by sending family and friends loving thoughts every time you think of them. Be honest with yourself and others in a loving way. Forgive everyone you feel has ever harmed or hurt you. *Let it go.* Most important, forgive yourself. The past is over, and the present is a clean page ready to become your masterpiece. Affirm: *"I am strong and vibrant in body, heart, mind, and spirit. I honor and respect myself by setting healthy boundaries. I completely forgive myself and others for past occurrences, and send loving, healing thoughts to all of my relations. I enjoy a healthy, honest, loving relationship with myself and all of my friends and family members."*

Enhance the Health and Family Area When:

◈   your health needs a boost;

◈   you're planning or recovering from a medical procedure;

◈   you would like your relationship with relatives to improve;

◈   you're beginning, or already participating in, sports, dance, or exercise;

◈   you would like your social life and your "family of choice" to grow or improve; or

◈   you wish to strengthen the attributes of honesty and forgiveness.

Outer Enhancements Related to Health and Family:

- ⬧ Healthy plants with rounded leaves or a soft, graceful appearance
- ⬧ Fresh flowers
- ⬧ Dried or silk flowers and plants with a fresh, vibrant appearance
- ⬧ Artwork depicting your concept of ideal health
- ⬧ Posters and paintings of gardens and landscapes
- ⬧ Floral prints and stripes, including linens, wallpaper, and upholstery
- ⬧ Anything made from wood—such as tables, chairs, bowls, and vases
- ⬧ Pillars, columns, and pedestals
- ⬧ Photos of family and friends
- ⬧ Blues and greens
- ⬧ Quotes, sayings, and affirmations concerning honesty and forgiveness

Inner Work Related to Wealth and Prosperity

Key Word: *Gratitude*

Translated as "Persistent Wind," the I Ching trigram *Sun* is related to wealth and prosperity. In most cases, your wealth is accumulated over time, much as a tree is shaped by prevailing winds. To fully appreciate the magnitude of your wealth, cultivate an attitude of gratitude. Money is only one small part of your wealth and prosperity. You shape your life with all that you hold dear—from your close friends, family, and health, to your own burgeoning wisdom and talents. And, as with money, it's wise not to gamble with, or take for granted, your many gifts in life. The key to gathering and multiplying wealth is to persist in experiencing yourself as already blessed with abundant riches.

Wealth gathers around gratitude. Make a list of all of the people, places, and things you're grateful for; add to the list all of the qualities and talents you're blessed with. You now have a complete accounting of your wealth and prosperity. Notice how rich you are at this moment. As you focus on being grateful, aspects of your life will keep revealing themselves, adding to your "portfolio." Gratitude is your pathway to the steadfast experience of wealth and prosperity on every level. Read your list often, add to it, and revel in just how affluent you really are. Affirm: *"With joy and gratitude, I welcome an abundance of positive people and experiences into my life, now and always. I am rich and prosperous in every way, and blessed with a constant and abundant flow of health, wealth, and happiness."* Build your portfolio of wealth with gratitude, and your prosperity is assured.

Enhance the Wealth and Prosperity Area When:

- ⟡ you wish to generate more cash flow in your life;
- ⟡ you're raising money or resources for a special purpose; or
- ⟡ you would like to feel more grateful for the flow of abundance and prosperity in your life.

Outer Enhancements Related to Wealth and Prosperity:

- ⟡ Water features, especially when the water is moving
- ⟡ Wind chimes, prayer flags, and banners that symbolically call in wealth and prosperity
- ⟡ Beloved possessions and collections that are literally valuable, such as antiques, art, crystal, and coins
- ⟡ Posters, paintings, and photographs of the things you'd like to buy or experience
- ⟡ All blues, purples, and reds
- ⟡ Sayings, quotes, and affirmations related to gratitude, wealth, and prosperity

Inner Work Related to Fame and Reputation

Key Word: *Integrity*

The I Ching trigram *Li,* representing Fame and Reputation, means "Clinging Fire." Like fire, your reputation has a way of clinging to you for a long time. A good reputation, earned by the steadfast practice of integrity, inspires good will and fans the flames for great things to happen. Bridges to good fortune are built in the clear light of integrity; while insincerity and dishonesty are quick to burn those bridges. For better or for worse, your words and actions are remembered, and often exaggerated, long after they've been said and done. Be mindful of what you're famous for because it will cling to you for a long time.

This is true whether or not anyone else knows about your miscue; the one person you want to establish an impeccable reputation with most is *yourself.* When you're accountable in thought, word, and deed, you illuminate your path through life. Evaluate your level of integrity. For instance, do you consider yourself a person of sound character? Do you keep your word? Only you know how honest you really are. Let any act of insincerity or dishonesty become a thing of the past, and practice "being your word." It's your integrity that builds and strengthens your reputation, and cultivates the priceless rewards of self-respect and self-esteem. Affirm: *"My integrity inspires good will and good fortune. I am trustworthy in all that I say and do."*

Enhance the Fame and Reputation Area When:

⊕   you would like more recognition at work or at home;

⊕   you wish to establish a good reputation in your community;

⊕   you would like to be well known for something you do; or

⊕   you wish to raise your level of integrity.

Outer Enhancements Related to Fame and Reputation:

- ✧ Symbols of your accomplishments, such as diplomas, awards, certificates, or trophies

- ✧ Pleasant lighting

- ✧ Artwork that depicts people or animals

- ✧ Items that are made from animals, such as leather, feathers, silk, and wool

- ✧ Images of people you respect

- ✧ Symbols of your goals for the future

- ✧ Objects or patterns that are triangular or conical in shape

- ✧ All subtle, bright, and deep shades of red

- ✧ Sayings, quotes, and affirmations relating to integrity, and to your fame and reputation

Inner Work Related to Love and Marriage

Key Word: *Receptivity*

Love and Marriage are related to the I Ching Trigram *K'un,* which means "Receptive Earth." As the most Yin of all of the trigrams, this teaching encourages the cultivation of receptivity and unconditional love. To truly receive love, you must open your heart and be entirely receptive to your partner. The *armor* falls away in the presence of *amour.* Successful intimate love relationships thrive when both partners trust each other completely and give and receive from each other with open hearts. All happy couples know how gentle, loving, and sweet they can be in their intimate moments together—these are all Yin qualities, and they make the difference between an ordinary and an extraordinary love life.

Perhaps the most important intimate relationship you can cultivate is the one with yourself. Treat yourself with the same tender loving care you wish to receive from a lover. Be open to fulfilling your own needs, wishes, and aspirations. Your ability to love yourself enhances your Ch'i, cultivates your magnetism, and attracts loving people to you. Take yourself on dates to places you love, create a romantic mood, and allow your own deepest rhythms to emerge and be celebrated. Being single gives you time to explore and develop your unique talents and interests. Take classes and tours, join special interest groups, volunteer to help others. Singlehood is a window of opportunity to craft your life exactly the way you wish it to be and to love the one person you'll know most intimately for a lifetime—yourself. Look in the mirror and say: *"You are a magnificent person. I love and cherish you completely, now and always."*

Enhance the Love and Marriage Area When:

◈ you would like to attract a romantic relationship;

◈ you wish to improve the romantic relationship you have now;

◈ you're developing or enriching a loving relationship with yourself; or

◈ you wish to be more openhearted and receptive.

Outer Enhancements Related to Love and Marriage:

◈ Artwork portraying romance and love

◈ Pairs of things, such as candlesticks, flowers, books, and statues

◈ Mementos from romantic experiences

◈ Favorite photographs of you, or you and your true love

◈ Items in reds, pinks, and white

◈ Quotes, sayings, and affirmations on love and romance

Inner Work Related to Children and Creativity

Key Word: *Joy*

The I Ching trigram *Tui,* meaning "Joyous Lake," is associated with the Children and Creativity area of the Bagua Map and the attributes of joy and encouragement. We're all creators in life—to live is to create, and to create is to be truly alive. The key to entering fully into the creative process is *joy.* The joy and pleasure you take in your everyday creations connects you with the joy of all creation. A child's natural ability to spontaneously create art, plays, songs, poems, dances, skits, games, and music erupts from the joy of being alive. It's the pure childlike quality of joy within you that imbues you with the creative spirit.

Take every opportunity to encourage your creativity. Spend time with creative people, go to art galleries, "artfully" express your goals and dreams. Buy a big box of crayons or colored pencils, and let your creative spirit flow. Stir a new spice into your soup. Nurture yourself and others with large helpings of encouragement so that creativity flourishes all around you. Let children and adults alike know how wonderful their creative works are, even when their skies are orange, their chimneys are crooked, their trees look like lollipops, and their people have three arms—in the spirit of joyful creativity, it's perfect! The I Ching suggests that when you encourage the creativity in people to come out and play, you enlighten the world with joy.

Think of some of the creative experiences you've had. In the best of all possible worlds, your creativity was supported and encouraged every step of the way by an enthusiastic fan club of friends, family, and mentors who said, "Wow, good work!" and "That's so beautiful!" If not, you may have felt vulnerable and discouraged when your creative work was met with "What an awful color!" "It's not the right shape!" or "It certainly needs salt." Whether you've been encouraged to be creative or not, take stock of your daily creative expressions. Whether it's dressing imaginatively or telling stories to your children, any action can be creative, depending on how you approach it.

Step into being the enthusiastic creator of harmony, health, and beauty

188

in your environment. Stimulate your creative juices by doing things that really turn you on. Awaken your creative genius by letting your inner child come out and play. Turn the music up in your living room, and move to the beat. Sing at the top of your lungs in the car. Get good and dirty in the garden. Do as much of what fills you with joy as possible—for ultimately, you are your own greatest fan. Nurture your inner environment with joy, encouragement, and delight. Affirm: "*I experience great joy and pleasure in creatively expressing myself. I attract joyful, fun people who encourage me to be creative. The more I express myself creatively, the happier I am.*"

Enhance the Children and Creativity Area When:

◈ you wish to be more creative in any way;

◈ you're involved in a creative project;

◈ you feel creatively blocked;

◈ you wish to explore and develop your inner-child qualities;

◈ you would like to improve your relationship with children;

◈ you would like to become pregnant; or

◈ you wish to experience more joy.

Outer Enhancements Related to Children and Creativity:

◈ Art or objects that are especially creative, whimsical, playful, or colorful, or that stimulate your creative juices

◈ Toys, dolls, and stuffed animals that bring you joy

◈ Photographs of children, along with anything made by hand

◈ Rocks and stones

◈ Circular and oval shapes

◈ Items made from metal

◈ Items in white or light pastels

◈ Quotes, sayings, and affirmations about joy, children, and creativity

Inner Work Related to Helpful People and Travel

Key Word: *Synchronicity*

The Helpful People and Travel area is associated with the I Ching trigram *Ch'ien*, meaning "Heaven." This is the most Yang of all of the trigrams, and is associated with clarity, synchronicity, and right action. You create "Heaven on Earth" when you focus clearly on what you want to accomplish, and then take action accordingly, letting synchronicity be your guide. Think of a time when your life was transformed by a helpful person or special place: Perhaps you met someone who became your mentor, or you were traveling in a place that awakened a lost memory. Touched by the experience of synchronicity, you found yourself in the right place, meeting the right people, at just the right time. When you experience the people in your life as angels, and the places where you live, work, and play as paradises, you're "in sync." The opposite experience, replete with its devilish people and punishing places, clearly tells you that you need to reset your path. You know you're back on track when the angelic people and heavenly experiences reappear to show you the way, just like divine signposts. Cultivate clarity of mind, heart, and spirit; set your intentions; focus upon them; say no to what doesn't match, and yes to what does. In this way, heavenly moments expand into hours, days, weeks . . . a lifetime.

As with any powerful change, transforming your present state of being can take tremendous focus and action. Decide to be your own angel—create your own heavenly place and let synchronicity be your guide. Affirm: "*I attract the perfect people, places, and things into my life every day. I am always in the right place and with the right people at the right time. My destiny unfolds with ease and grace.*"

Enhance the Helpful People and Travel Area When:

⊕   you wish to attract more mentors, clients, customers, employees, colleagues—helpful people of any description—into your life;

⊕   you wish to travel in general, or to a particular place;

⊕   you would like to feel more connected to your spiritual or religious belief system—which may be considered the ultimate "helpful people";

⊕   you're moving to a new home or work location; or

⊕   you wish to experience more synchronicity.

Outer Enhancements Related to Helpful People and Travel:

⊕   Art that depicts religious or spiritual figures you love, such as angels, saints, goddesses, and teachers

⊕   Objects that have personal spiritual associations, such as a rosary, a crystal, or a book of prayers

⊕   Photographs of people who have been helpful to you, such as mentors, teachers, or relatives

⊕   Art, posters, and collages of places you'd like to visit or live, or that are special to you

⊕   Items in white, gray, and black

⊕   Quotes, sayings, and affirmations on miracles, heavenly experiences, and synchronicity

Inner Work Related to Career

Key Word: *Courage*

The I Ching trigram associated with your life's work or career is *K'an,* meaning "Deep Water." Many of us know how unsettling it can be to decide on a career path. Like it or not, we're swept into our own depths as we explore a potential vocation. Once chosen, the path can be mysterious, often leading to unforeseen challenges, and yes, even more changes: The lawyer becomes a chef, and then a kitchen designer—after which he retires and goes into politics; the housewife becomes an image consultant, then an artist, business owner, and teacher. At every turn in your career path, you're summoned back into the deep waters within to explore the unfolding of your destiny. You may find yourself questioning the profession you once loved, or discovering that you wish to follow an entirely different career path. This can be a difficult experience that includes making choices that others disagree with. Your courage is crucial—you need to be ready, willing, and able to listen to your inner voice, and follow it. Joseph Campbell called it "following your bliss." Ultimately, you know best the career path that calls to you, so go for it!

When you find yourself in a quandary about your vocation, consider taking time away from your daily schedule to do some inner exploration. Go on a vision quest, retreat, or camping trip, even if it's only for a few days. Once you're away from it all, open yourself to receiving your next set of life instructions: Watch your dreams; keep a journal; define your purpose in life; and make drawings, collages, or lists on what you love to do. Give voice to parts of yourself that aren't directly linked to producing an income. Stir the pot. Maintain your courage and trust yourself. Affirm: *"I am completely open to fulfilling my destiny. In so being, my work in the world becomes more fulfilling, inspiring, and lucrative every day."*

Enhance the Career Area When:

- ⊕ you're seeking your purpose in life;
- ⊕ you wish to make a change in your current job or career;
- ⊕ you wish to volunteer or do meaningful community service work;
- ⊕ you're moving from one vocation to another; or
- ⊕ you wish to be more courageous.

Outer Enhancements Related to Career:

- ⊕ Water features, such as fountains, waterfalls, and aquariums
- ⊕ Artwork or photos depicting bodies of water, such as pools, streams, lakes, or the ocean
- ⊕ Any image or object that personally symbolizes your career, such as books on your subject of expertise, or items with your company name
- ⊕ Items that are free-form, flowing, or asymmetrically shaped
- ⊕ Mirrors, crystals, and glass items
- ⊕ Items in black or very dark tones
- ⊕ Quotes, sayings, and affirmations related to courage and following one's path in life

Inner Work Related to Knowledge and Self-Cultivation

Key Word: *Stillness*

The I Ching's trigram *Ken,* meaning "Still Mountain," is associated with knowledge and self-cultivation. You absorb knowledge best, whether in school or in life, when you allow your body and mind to be still on a regular basis. The mountain symbolizes climbing to a peaceful inner space where you can assimilate and integrate your daily experiences. Stillness, the Yin counterpart to Yang action, transforms your knowledge and adventures into wisdom. To be wise, you need quiet time to balance your active time. When you build quietude into your daily routine, you honor the full rhythm of life. This teaching reminds us all-too-busy Westerners that to be truly brilliant, creative, and productive, we must also embrace stillness.

Give yourself a daily gift of stillness. If you're not already practicing some form of meditation, introspection, or contemplation, begin now. There are literally hundreds of books and classes on how to quiet the mind and body. Some people find that it's easier to be still after some physical activity, such as dancing or exercising. If you're a beginner, start with five minutes twice a day, every day. You can begin now by sitting comfortably and watching your breath for a few moments. Focus on your inhalation and exhalation, and simply sit and *breathe,* refocusing on your breath whenever your attention wanders. By taking a time-out from being active every waking moment, you deepen the peace and wisdom residing within you. Affirm: *"I am wise and calm. In stillness, I deepen my inner peace and wisdom."*

Enhance the Knowledge and Self-Cultivation Area When:

- you're a student of any subject at any time;

- you're in counseling or engaged in any self-growth activity; or

- you wish to cultivate wisdom and peace of mind.

Outer Enhancements Related to Knowledge and Self-Cultivation:

- Books, tapes, or other material that you're currently studying

- Art that portrays mountains or quiet places, such as meditation gardens

- Pictures or photographs of people you consider accomplished and wise

- Items in the colors of black, blue, or green

- Meditative and inspirational sayings, quotes, or affirmations

Inner Work Related to the Center

The Center of the Bagua Map is considered the hub of the wheel, or the home's "solar plexus." The element of Earth finds a home here, symbolizing the importance of arranging our lives to flow around a solid, grounded base. Many traditional Chinese homes had a central earthen courtyard where Earth Ch'i was directly available to the inhabitants. If there's space in the Center of your home, it's an excellent location for a courtyard, atrium, or potted plants. Otherwise, you can display art that reminds you to stay centered and connected with the earth. Because of its association with the earth, ceramics and yellow and earthtone colors can also enhance the Center of your home.

Determine how grounded and connected to your Center you feel at this time. Nurture your ability to remain centered through life's many changes by directly connecting with the earth every day. Take a walk; sit on the grass, sand, or dirt; or literally put your hands in the soil by working in a garden. Watch how your inner being becomes stronger and more centered as you connect with the earth. Affirm: *"I remain grounded and centered all the time. I am always in the secure and loving embrace of Mother Earth."*

Bagua Map Exercise

Collect images that depict the Bagua area(s) you're working with, such as those of your ideal partner, job, family, health or financial situation, and make them into a collage. When you express yourself creatively, you're literally gathering Ch'i to enhance your life. You can draw, paint, weave, build, or sculpt images that symbolize your goals. Ask yourself questions, such as: *What color is my health? What shape is my reputation? What images do I associate with my career?* Surprisingly powerful answers can come from this process. Your own art strikes a very personal chord as the tangible expression of your inner quest. Be sure to display it, if only temporarily, so that your chosen images can nurture and sustain your goals.

Appendix II

Yin and Yang and the Five Elements— Nature's Abundant Palette

Yin and Yang

As human beings, we seek the perfect balance between environmental extremes—such as cold and hot, dark and light, or small and large. In Feng Shui, these extremes are defined as either *Yin* or *Yang*. One extreme, Yin, is associated with curved shapes and small, cold, dark, wet, or ornate settings and items. Yang, the other extreme, is associated with angular shapes and large, light, hot, or open settings and items. Feng Shui observes that the more extreme our home designs are, the more uncomfortable they may feel to us. People tend to be happiest and most comfortable with a balanced mix of Yin and Yang features in their environments.

Western architecture and design is often quite Yang, with a plethora of angles, high ceilings, large pieces of furniture, huge windows, and sharp corners. In the midst of this, it's easy to see why Feng Shui practitioners often suggest softer, rounder, more Yin shapes and furnishings to balance those Yang environments. We may love high ceilings, huge white expanses, and bright lights in our art galleries, churches, and shopping malls, but at some point, we're ready to return to the cozy, comfortable place we call *home*, where everything's just right.

Although our culture tends to lean toward Yang architecture, the Yin extreme can also be found. Picture a small and dark room, with heavy furniture, dim lighting, and a low ceiling. Many basements are like this. Yang components, such as additional lighting, large mirrors, and warm, light colors are needed to balance the many Yin features in such a room. Much more common is the room that's large and angular, with a high ceiling, white walls, big windows, sizable art pieces, and light-colored furniture. Here, Yin components, such as rounded tables, ornate upholstery and window treatments, soft rugs, and dark, rich colors are needed to create balance and comfort.

The balance of each room in your home needs to be approached individually. A bedroom can be quite Yin—soft duvets, ornate patterns, fluffy pillows, low lighting—and still be comfortable, because the function of rest and rejuvenation is primarily Yin. Even so, there should always be a balance. Too many pillows, too many little bottles on the bureau, and too many layers of lace and fabric can tilt the balance. On the other hand, Yang components—such as a large desk, bright lights, and business equipment—in a home office can be just what you need to get the job done. Just keep in mind that too many sharp angles and hard surfaces can promote irritation and stress.

When Yin and Yang are balanced, you experience each room in your home as comfortable and beautiful—a personal paradise that both functions well and nourishes and protects your health, happiness, and prosperity.

The Five Elements

In Feng Shui, the elements Wood, Fire, Earth, Metal, and Water are considered the basic building blocks of everything physical on the planet. They manifest in countless ways and combinations all around us. Feng Shui observes that human beings are made up of all Five Elements, and therefore, we're most comfortable when they're all present in our homes. The fastest way to learn how to work with the elements is to observe them in your own environment.

The Five Elements

controlling ----->
nourishing ----->

fire

wood

earth

water

metal

Figure IIA: *The Five Elements.*

Although many people can sense when their surroundings are out of balance, they often don't know exactly how to fix the problem. *Would red or blue be good here? Should the table be round or rectangular? Is a mirror or artwork best there?* Questions such as these are easily answered when you know how to read the elements, making them some of your most intriguing Feng Shui tools. Learn how to recognize and combine the Five Elements, and you'll be able to see exactly what each room needs to bring it into perfect balance.

THE FIVE ELEMENTS
Nourishing and Controlling Relationships

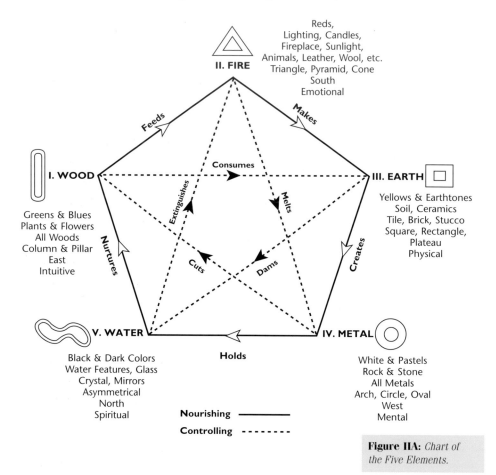

Reds,
Lighting, Candles,
Fireplace, Sunlight,
Animals, Leather, Wool, etc.
Triangle, Pyramid, Cone
South
Emotional

II. FIRE

Feeds

Makes

Consumes

I. WOOD

Extinguishes

Melts

III. EARTH

Greens & Blues
Plants & Flowers
All Woods
Column & Pillar
East
Intuitive

Nurtures

Cuts

Dams

Creates

Yellows & Earthtones
Soil, Ceramics
Tile, Brick, Stucco
Square, Rectangle,
Plateau
Physical

V. WATER

Holds

IV. METAL

Black & Dark Colors
Water Features, Glass
Crystal, Mirrors
Asymmetrical
North
Spiritual

White & Pastels
Rock & Stone
All Metals
Arch, Circle, Oval
West
Mental

Nourishing ——————

Controlling - - - - - - -

Figure IIA: *Chart of the Five Elements.*

An Overall Elemental Reading

To determine the overall elemental balance of a room, use the following lists of associations related to the Five Elements. Pay attention to the things made out of the elements themselves, such as wooden or metal furnishings. Find those items that are associated with an element, such as a marble tabletop (Metal), a mirror (Water), or plants (Wood). Look for colors associated with each element, such as red (Fire), blues and greens (Wood), or yellow (Earth). Note that the darker a color gets, the more "Watery" it becomes—such as black, navy blue, and dark brown; while the lighter a color gets, the more it becomes associated with Metal. Look at your artwork to see what element it portrays, such as a "Fiery" sunset painting or a "Watery" oceanscape. Take an overall reading, and observe whether there are elements that dominate, are barely represented, or are missing entirely from the room.

In "Soap and Mirrors" (page 19), Cynthia helped Gary artfully balance the elements and improve the Helpful People and Travel area of his store [see Figure 3B, page 23]. The bright red fireplace brought in an abundance of the Fire element; Metal was strongly represented by the white fireplace cover, mantel, and trim. With Fire and Metal in place, Cynthia made suggestions that would specifically introduce Earth, Water, and Wood into the environment. As a result, Gary removed a display of candles (Fire), added a water fountain (Water), and a wreath and an abundant flower and fruit display in earthy colors (Wood and Earth). This arrangement brought all five elements into a vibrantly pleasing balance that has served him well.

Each element has a wide assortment of associations and qualities that can enrich your environment, especially when you work to balance them in a personally pleasing manner.

1. The Wood Element

Energetically, the Wood element "grows and branches out" to foster intuition, creativity, flexibility, and expansion. When there's too much Wood in an environment, it can promote a sense of being overwhelmed or over-committed, while too little Wood can stagnate growth and impede intuitive and creative flow.

The Wood element is found in:

- wooden furniture, paneling, and accessories;

- all plants and flowers—including silk, plastic, and dried plants;

- plant-based cloth and textiles, such as cotton and rayon;

- floral upholstery, wall coverings, draperies, and linens;

- art portraying landscapes, gardens, plants, and flowers;

- columnar shapes—such as pillars, pedestals, and poles;

- paper;

- stripes; and

- blue and green tones.

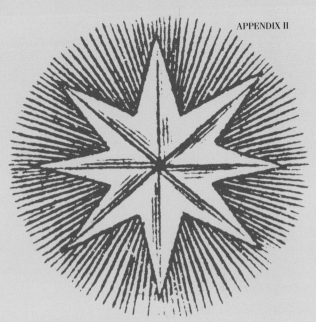

2. The Fire Element

The Fire element energetically "warms and expands," activating leadership qualities and kindling healthy emotional interactions between people. Too much Fire in an environment stimulates or amplifies aggression, impatience, and impulsive behavior, while too little Fire can promote emotional darkness or coldness.

The Fire element is found in:

- lighting—including electric, oil, candles, fireplaces, and natural sunlight;
- items from animals—such as leather, feathers, silk, and wool;
- pets and wildlife;
- art portraying people or animals;
- art depicting sunshine, fire, or other illumination;
- triangles, pyramids, and cone shapes; and
- all red tones—including pink, red-orange, magenta, and maroon.

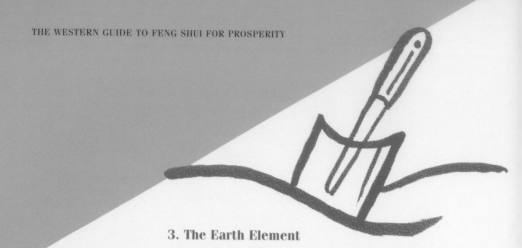

3. The Earth Element

Energetically, the Earth element "grounds and sustains," which enhances physical strength, sensuality, order, practicality, and stability. Too much Earth in a home creates an atmosphere that's quite heavy, serious, or conservative; too little of the Earth element promotes instability, clutter, and chaos.

The Earth element is found in:

- adobe, brick, and tile;

- ceramics and earthenware objects;

- square and rectangular shapes;

- art portraying earthy landscapes—such as deserts or fertile fields; and

- yellow and all earthtones.

4. The Metal Element

The Metal element energetically "contracts" to enhance mental acuity and strengthen presence of mind, even in times of stress. Too much Metal creates mental rigidity, stubbornness, lack of teamwork, and the inability to compromise; too little Metal promotes indecisiveness, procrastination, mental dullness, and confusion.

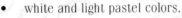

The Metal element is found in:

- all metals—including stainless steel, copper, brass, iron, silver, aluminum, and gold;

- cement, rocks, and stones—including marble, granite, and flagstone;

- natural crystals and gemstones;

- art and sculpture made from metal or stone;

- circular, oval, and arched shapes; and

- white and light pastel colors.

5. The Water Element

Energetically, the Water element "flows," enhancing spirituality, inspiration, relaxation, and cooperation. Too much Water in an environment can promote lack of direction and diminish grounded productivity, while too little encourages stress, rivalry, anxiety, pettiness, and sarcasm.

The Water element is found in:

- streams, pools, fountains, and water features of all kinds;

- reflective surfaces—such as cut crystal, glass, and mirrors;

- flowing, free-form, and asymmetrical shapes;

- art portraying bodies of water; and

- black and all dark tones—such as charcoal gray and navy blue.

Artful Elemental Combinations

As you learn to identify the Five Elements, you'll notice that there are many things that combine several, or even all, of them. An aquarium, traditionally favored in Feng Shui for its Ch'i-enhancing qualities, gathers all of the elements together in one lively arrangement. It's just one of countless ways in which you can harmoniously bring all of the elements together. Judith created a five-element arrangement in "Practice Makes Perfect" (page 93). She arranged a small water fountain (Water), polished stone (Metal), candle (Fire), and terracotta figures (Earth and Fire) on a wooden credenza (Wood). She purposefully arranged these items to welcome clients as they step in the door of her husband's office.

Five-element arrangements can be made in any room and can be any size that's appropriate for the space. I often suggest that people put together an elemental arrangement of objects in areas that need energizing, such as a garage, spare bedroom, or basement. This positive action marks the beginning of change and stimulates the Ch'i so that it's easier for people to organize these areas.

The Nourishing Cycle of the Five Elements

When you balance the Five Elements in a room, you're tapping into the Nourishing Cycle, where each element feeds and sustains the others in perfect harmony. If you refer to the pentagon portion of the Five Element Chart [see Figures IIA and IIB], you can see that Water sustains Wood; Wood feeds Fire; Fire makes Earth; Earth creates Metal; and Metal holds Water. The Nourishing Cycle shows us how the elements strengthen and nurture each other in an endless regenerating sequence—when all five are present in an environment, a natural balance is achieved.

The Controlling Cycle of the Five Elements

In the Controlling Cycle—the star-shaped portion of the Five Element Chart—we see how the elements dominate and control each other. In this cycle, Wood consumes Earth; Earth dams Water; Water extinguishes Fire; Fire melts Metal; and Metal cuts Wood. The Controlling Cycle is regarded as a powerful guide for establishing elemental harmony and is present in many of the places we consider the most beautiful. A palm tree oasis in the desert is a perfect example of Wood consuming Earth, while a tropical island in crystal-clear water is essentially Earth damming Water. Nature constantly provides us with examples of how the Controlling Cycle of the elements can create harmony and beauty.

It's also very useful to be aware of the Controlling Cycle when you're balancing the elements in your home. When one element is especially dominant, the Controlling Cycle will show you the element that can quickly balance the Ch'i. Once you've balanced the dominant element with its controlling partner, you can turn to the Nourishing Cycle and further refine your elemental work.

When Holly first saw Nick's office in "Gone Fishin'" (page 1), she noted that the overabundance of the Fire element was matched by Nick's aggressive, impatient behavior. To elementally balance his environment, she suggested the removal of some of the fiery decor and the addition of Fire's controlling element—Water—via photographs of water and a tabletop fountain. To enhance the office's Metal element, Holly suggested that the water fountain be made out of that element. Wood was strengthened with plants, while the Earth element was represented by the gold walls and rectangular shape of the desk. When the five elements were balanced, Nick was able to calm down and enjoy achieving his goals.

Elemental extremes abound in our architecture and rooms. Monochromatic motifs and the constant repetition of one shape are two things we often see in homes and workplaces. Although the effect may be perceived as quite trendy or dramatic, most people won't find comfort there, for on the elemental level, it's imbalanced. Remember, your ultimate goal is to bring all Five Elements into balance in every room. As with Nick, it's remarkable to witness the difference this makes in the perceived comfort of a space and in the personalities of the people living or working there.

A Quick Reference for Working with the Controlling Cycle

When the dominating element is Wood:
Bring in the Controlling element of Metal,
Highlight with Earth and Fire,
Refine as needed with touches of Water.

When the dominant element is Fire:
Bring in the Controlling element of Water,
Highlight with Metal and Earth,
Refine as needed with touches of Wood.

When the dominant element is Earth:
Bring in the Controlling element of Wood,
Highlight with Water and Metal,
Refine as needed with touches of Fire.

When the dominant element is Metal:
Bring in the Controlling element of Fire,
Highlight with Wood and Water,
Refine as needed with touches of Earth.

When the dominant element is Water:
Bring in the Controlling element of Earth,
Highlight with Fire and Wood,
Refine as needed with touches of Metal.

Elemental Fluency

Practice identifying the Five Elements, and study their interplay in your home, your friends' homes, restaurants, stores, and in your workplace. As you do, you're learning a vital part of Feng Shui alchemy. There's a magical moment when you realize that you've become fluent in a language that benefits you and everyone around you. And from that point forward, you'll be able to create environments that are balanced and vibrant in every way.

Recommended Reading

Adventures of a Feng Shui Detective, Valmai Howe Elkins. Montreal, Canada. Woodley & Watts, 1999.

Clear Your Clutter with Feng Shui, Karen Kingston. New York, NY. Broadway Books, 1998.

Clutter's Last Stand, Don Aslett. Cincinnati, OH. Writer's Digest Books, 1984.

Creating Sacred Space with Feng Shui, Karen Kingston. New York, NY. Broadway Books, 1997.

Cultivating Sacred Space: Gardening for the Soul, Elizabeth Murray. Rohnert Park, CA. Pomegranate, 1997.

Dressing The Whole Person (book and workbook), Evana Maggiore, AICI. Woburn, MA. Mansion Publishing LTD., 1998.

The Dynamic Laws of Prosperity, Catherine Ponder. Marina del Rey, CA. DeVorss & Co, 1973.

Feng Shui at Home, Carol Soucek King. New York, NY. St. Martin's Press, 1999.

Feng Shui Chic, Sharon Stasney. New York, NY. Sterling Publishers, 2000.

Feng Shui Design, Sarah Rossbach and Lin Yun. New York, NY. Viking, 1998.

Feng Shui for the Soul, Denise Linn. Carlsbad, CA. Hay House, Inc., 1999.

Feng Shui In Your Garden, Roni Jay. Boston, MA. Tuttle, 1998.

Feng Shui Made Easy, William Spear. New York, NY. HarperCollins, 1995.

Feng Shui Revealed, R.D. Chin. New York, NY. Clarkson Potter Publishers, 1998.

The Handbook of Chinese Horoscopes, Theodora Lau. New York, NY. Harper & Row, 1998.

Healing Environments, Carol Venolia. Berkeley, CA. Celestial Arts, 1998.

The Healing House, Barbara Bannon Harwood. Carlsbad, CA. Hay House, Inc., 1997.

Home Design with Feng Shui A-Z, Terah Kathryn Collins. Carlsbad, CA. Hay House, Inc., 1999.

A Home for the Soul, Anthony Lawlor. New York, NY. Clarkson Potter Publishers, 1997.

Home Harmony, Suzy Chiazzari. North Pomfret, VT. Trafalgar Square Publishing, 2001.

House As a Mirror of Self, Clare Cooper Marcus. Berkeley, CA. Conari Press, 1995.

How to Grow Fresh Air, Dr. B.C. Wolverton. New York, NY. Penguin Books, 1997.

The I Ching or Book of Changes, Richard Wilhelm & Carey Baynes. Princeton, NJ. Princeton, University Press, 1971.

The Illustrated I Ching, R.L. Wing. New York, NY. Doubleday, 1982.

Interior Design with Feng Shui, Sarah Rossbach. Toronto, Canada. Arkana Books, 1997.

Light, Radiation & You, John N. Ott. Greenwich, CT. Devin-Adder Publishers, 1990.

Living Color, Sarah Rossbach & Lin Yun. New York, NY. Kodansha International, 1994.

Make Room For Joy, Susan L. Colantuono. Charleston, RI. Interlude Productions, 2000.

Multicultural Feng Shui, Maureen L. Belle. Greenbank, WA. White Doe Productions, 2001.

A Pattern Language, Christopher Alexander. New York, NY. Oxford University Press, 1977.

Sacred Space, Denise Linn. New York, NY. Ballantine Books, 1995.

The Sensual Home, Isle Crawford. New York, NY. Rizzoli International Publishers, 1998.

Shelter for Spirit, Victoria Moran. New York, NY. HarperCollins Publishers, 1997.

Shower of Jewels, Richard The-Fu Tan, O.M.D.L.Ac and Cheryl Warnke, L.Ac. San Diego, CA. T & W Books, 1996.

A Soul in Place, Carol Bridges. Nashville, IN. Earth Nation Publishing, 1995.

Space Clearing, Denise Linn. London, England. Ebury Press, 2000.

Space Clearing A-Z, Denise Linn. Carlsbad, CA. Hay House, Inc., 2001.

The Temple in the House, Anthony Lawlor, AIA. New York, NY. Penguin Putnam, 1994.

The Timeless Way of Building, Christopher Alexander. New York, NY. Oxford University Press, 1979.

Traditional Acupuncture: The Law of the Five Elements, Diane M. Connelly, Ph.D., M.Ac., Columbia, MD. Self Published, Traditional Acupuncture Institute, 1994

The Western Guide to Feng Shui: Creating Balance, Harmony, and Prosperity in Your Environment, Terah Kathryn Collins. Carlsbad, CA. Hay House, Inc., 1996.

The Western Guide to Feng Shui: Room by Room, Terah Kathryn Collins. Carlsbad, CA. Hay House, Inc., 1999.

You Can Have it All, Arnold M. Patent. Hillsboro, OR. Beyond Words Publishing, 1995.

You Can Heal Your Life, Louise L. Hay. Carlsbad, CA. Hay House, Inc., 1987.

About the Author

Terah Kathryn Collins is an internationally recognized Feng Shui author, consultant, speaker, and teacher. Her first book, *The Western Guide to Feng Shui: Creating Balance, Harmony, and Prosperity in Your Environment,* is one of the bestselling Feng Shui books in the world and has been translated into eight languages. Her second book, *Home Design with Feng Shui, A–Z,* is a colorfully illustrated quick reference guide; while her third, *The Western Guide to Feng Shui: Room by Room,* contains more than 100 photographs on the subject. Terah's *Feng Shui Personal Paradise Cards* feature an informative booklet and 54 colorful flash cards that explain all of the Feng Shui basics.

Terah is the founder of the Western School of Feng Shui in Solana Beach, California, and the originator of Essential Feng Shui®, which focuses on the many practical applications Feng Shui has to offer our Western culture. Featured on the PBS *Body and Soul* series, Terah has spoken at numerous special events, including the New Millennium Conference in Mexico, Magical Mastery and Today's Wisdom Tours in Australia, and the Empowering Women Conferences across the United States.

Whether you want to transform your residence into a personal paradise, your office into a powerhouse of productivity, or you're searching for a rewarding new career, Western School of Feng Shui can light your way. We offer:

- ❖ Practitioner Training
- ❖ Essential Feng Shui® Workshops
- ❖ Professional Consultations for Residences and Business
- ❖ Feng Shui Speakers for Group Presentations
- ❖ Feng Shui Products at the "Essential Feng Shui Gallery"

WESTERN SCHOOL OF FENG SHUI™
Terah Kathryn Collins, Founder

More Results, Less Mystery
Essential Feng Shui® Practitioner Training Program

Since 1996, Western School of Feng Shui has offered training for men and women who are interested in becoming practitioners or who want to add Feng Shui to their current career. This unique and practical program is founded upon the principles presented in Terah's books. The training is for anyone who feels committed to enrich his or her life, or who wants to embark on a nurturing and rewarding full-time or part-time career path.

"Feng Shui Marketing" is included as a vital component of the training, enabling graduates to turn their knowledge into tangible real-world success. Students and graduates have the opportunity to participate in optional programs designed to support a prosperous Feng Shui practice, including a mentor program, speakers bureau, workshop presentation opportunities, consultation referrals, online directory listing and chat room, alumni networking, newsletters, and advanced training programs.

"This is the most comprehensive Feng Shui training that I've found. I feel confident, and my clients are seeing the results."

— Pamela K. Greer, Del Mar, CA

Visit us at **www.wsfs.com**, or call **800-300-6785** for more information.
Or, write to :
Western School of Feng Shui
437 South Highway 101, Suite 752
Solana Beach, CA 92075

Western School of Feng Shui draws students from across the United States and from more than 26 countries. The commitment they share and the camaraderie they enjoy add a rich dimension to a learning environment filled with intellectual and creative stimulation.

Professional Consultation Services
for Your Residence, Business, or Organization

Wherever you live or work in the United States or abroad, we can bring the benefits of Feng Shui to your doorstep by referring a seasoned professional Practitioner who is a graduate of Western School of Feng Shui. Our Practitioners are dedicated to getting results while honoring your personal style and taste.

A consultation for your residence can create positive changes in health, relationships, and prosperity—and improve the behavior of children.

"Since Kathryn Voreis came into my life, I have had a much stronger relationship with my husband and we have learned to work together as a team. My career path was finally clarified, resulting in my writing and producing my first book, and now it's distributed by a major bookstore. I definitely believe Feng Shui influenced my life."

— V.G., Fort Worth, TX

A consultation for your business can enhance productivity and profits, reduce stress, improve synergy and creativity, and improve employee retention.

"When Holly Tashian came into my office and suggested a few simple changes and rearrangements, I was absolutely amazed at the results. What followed was an unbelievable succession of events—large orders, big reviews, checks in the mail, surprising good news via phone calls and, seemingly out of nowhere, we attracted the interest of a large-scale group in New York."

— M.M, Nashville, TN

Consultation for organizations and institutions can increase efficiency, reduce employee turnover and sick leave, help prevent burnout, and improve morale.

"Since Shivam Kohls came to our nonprofit organization for a Feng Shui consultation, many wonderful things have happened: Within weeks we received over $10K in donations, the county has contacted us about starting our program in other locations, and our morale is up like never before. All this happened with only minor changes and minimal expense. Thank you!"

— Alan Sorkin, Executive Director, PARTS
(Parents and Adolescents Recovering Together Successfully), San Diego, CA

Find a Feng Shui Practitioner in your area at **www.wsfs.com,** or call
800-300-6785 for a referral (local: **858-793-0945**).

ENJOY A HANDS-ON FENG SHUI LEARNING EXPERIENCE

Feng Shui Essentials™—a Practical Workshop

This unique program is designed for beginning and intermediate students. It offers a powerful, practical approach to a subject often cloaked in mystery. It will deepen your basic knowledge of Feng Shui and give you tools that you can put into immediate use at home and at work. Our program, which includes a slide show with more than 100 images, is presented by skilled Feng Shui teachers and held throughout the U.S. and abroad. It is an excellent fundraising tool and is available to all organizations.

"Your workshop helped the members of our church understand new ways
to bring balance and harmony into our homes and offices—
and it helped us raise much-needed funds at a time when our
coffers were low. It was a brilliant, inspiring program!"

— L. Styler, Cleveland, OH

Visit **www.wsfs.com,** or call **800-300-6785** for information.

EMPOWER AND INSPIRE YOUR GROUP WITH A LIVE FENG SHUI PRESENTATION

Essential Feng Shui® Speakers Bureau

People in every company and organization are hungry for knowledge that can help them enjoy more healthy, happy, and productive lives. A live Feng Shui presentation arranged through our Speakers Bureau can fill this need by offering remarkable insights and practical tools that are tailored for your group. This is a subject that can captivate any audience, including: corporations, professional and trade organizations, spiritual groups, nonprofit groups, and educational and fraternal organizations. Our skilled presenters can tailor a presentation to fit the needs of your audience.

"Ellen Schneider of the Western School of Feng Shui Speakers Bureau did a remarkable job of communicating the value of Feng Shui to our business owners. We believe that this information will help our companies grow and prosper and help us all stay balanced in the process. Thanks again."

— Margy Campbell, National Association of
Women Business Owners, Salt Lake City Chapter

Visit **www.wsfs.com,** or call **800-300-6785** for information.

TREASURES AND TOOLS FOR ENHANCING YOUR LIFE

Essential Feng Shui® Gallery

To cultivate your interest in, or enhance your practice of, Feng Shui, Terah Kathryn Collins has personally selected a rich assortment of high-quality Feng Shui products, now available online through the Essential Feng Shui Gallery. These include:

• Books • Tapes • Gifts • Tools • Enhancements • Art

Please visit us at **www.wsfs.com** to view our growing list of offerings.

*Essential Feng Shui® is a registered trademark of
Western School of Feng Shui.*

Other Hay House Titles
of Related Interest

Books

FENG SHUI FOR THE SOUL, by Denise Linn

THE HEALING HOUSE:
How Living in the Right House Can Heal You
Spiritually, Emotionally, and Physically, by Barbara Bannon Harwood

SPACE CLEARING A–Z, by Denise Linn

Audio Programs

CLEAR YOUR CLUTTER WITH FENG SHUI, by Karen Kingston

All of the above are available at your local bookstore,
or may be ordered through Hay House, Inc.:

(800) 654-5126 or **(760) 431-7695**
(800) 650-5115 (fax) or **(760) 431-6948 (fax)**
www.hayhouse.com

We hope you enjoyed this Hay House book.
If you would like to receive a free catalog featuring additional
Hay House books and products, or if you would like information about the
Hay Foundation, please contact:

Hay House, Inc.
P.O. Box 5100
Carlsbad, CA 92018-5100

(760) 431-7695 or **(800) 654-5126**
(760) 431-6948 (fax) or **(800) 650-5115 (fax)**

Hay House Australia Pty Ltd
P.O. Box 515
Brighton-Le-Sands NSW 2216
phone: 1800 023 516
e-mail: info@hayhouse.com.au

Please visit the Hay House Website at: **www.hayhouse.com**